The 20th-Century Poster · Design of the Avant-Garde

POSTERS

by Dawn Ades

with contributions by
Robert Brown, Alma Law, Armin Hofmann
and Merrill C. Berman
Mildred Friedman, editor

Walker Art Center, Minneapolis

Abbeville Press
Publishers   New York

Major funding for this exhibition was provided by Champion International Corporation and the National Endowment for the Arts.

Presentation of the exhibition in Minneapolis was made possible by The McKnight Foundation, Herman Miller, Inc. and the Minnesota State Arts Board.

Library of Congress Cataloging in Publication Data

Ades, Dawn.
The 20th-Century Poster.

Bibliography: p. 207
Includes index.
1. Posters—History—20th century—Themes, motives.
I. Berman, Merrill C.
II. Walker Art Center.
III. Title.
IV. Title: Twentieth-century poster.
NC1815.A33   1984
741.67'4'0904
ISBN 0-89659-433-5
ISBN 0-89659-434-3 (pbk.)

Dimensions are in inches and centimeters; height precedes width. A paraphrase of each non-English poster text is provided.

(front cover)
Stenberg brothers
Battleship Potemkin 1905
1929, lithograph
[for Sovkino reissue of 1925 film by Goskino]
35⅜ x 26⅜, 90 x 67
Collection Merrill C. Berman

Director: Sergei Eisenstein
Cameraman: Eduard Tisse

(frontispiece)
A. M. Cassandre
L'Intransigeant
1925, lithograph
47¼ x 63, 120 x 160
Collection Merrill C. Berman

[A poster for a Parisian newspaper, designed to go on the newspaper's trucks, depicts Marianne, the "voice" of France, receiving the message through telegraphic wires, then delivering it through her mouth. "Les plus fort" is a shortened version of the newspaper's slogan, "Les plus fort tirage des journaux de soir" (The evening paper with the widest circulation).]

(back cover)
Niklaus Stoecklin
PKZ
1934, lithograph
50½ x 35⅝, 128.3 x 95
Courtesy Reinhold-Brown Gallery

Contents

VINCENT BROOKS, DAY & SON, L^{TD} LITH. LONDON. W.C.2

Broadside to Billboard

In art, 'content' is . . . the pretext, the goal, the lure which engages consciousness in essentially formal processes of transformation.

Susan Sontag, 1965

In the printed poster form and content are united, as the message is primary. Yet posters reflect many of the same philosophical and stylistic attitudes that underlie the more esoteric art forms, and on occasion their visual force transcends their practical function. For example, the 19th-century Japanese woodblock print that was used to advertise the Kabuki theater had a prodigious, lasting influence on the evolution of modern painting in the West. On the other hand, the 20th-century poster has often carried the spirit of the avant-garde into the cultural mainstream. The Beggarstaffs in England took the flat patterning of Post-Impressionism into the public realm in their remarkable advertisements for such commonplace products as Rowntree's Cocoa and *Harper's* magazine (p. 26). And twenty-five years later, while Europe was in the initial throes of revolutionary idealism, the search for words and pictures that would communicate to all was led by artists using abstract forms to create universal symbols. Dada proponents Theo van Doesburg and Kurt Schwitters made posters that presented their painterly conceptions in a more accessible format. At the same time the Russian constructivist painters El Lissitzky and Alexander Rodchenko used the poster to communicate the ideology of the new socialism in symbolic terms to a vast, largely unschooled Russian population.

Never intended as a unique or "precious" object, the poster has been the broad disseminator of the ideas and images that have characterized each period of modern history; it has directly mirrored social and cultural change, and in its most experimental periods, the poster has led the way to new forms—the traditional role of the avant-garde. In the 1920s, as the selling of products became more widespread and sophisticated, a number of artists devoted themselves almost exclusively to the creation of posters, thus securing a place for a new breed—the graphic designer.

(p. 6)
E. McKnight Kauffer
10 and 4, the Quiet Hours
1930, lithograph
40 x 25, 101.8 x 63.4
Collection Merrill C. Berman

Advances in design have been accompanied by technological developments that have gradually taken poster making from hand-printed to power-driven lithography to the computer-controlled press.

Through its metamorphosis from broadside to gigantic billboard, the poster has become a permanent part of the urban fabric, an ever changing pictorial background for the city street scene. Intended for pedestrians and occupants of slow moving vehicles, the early poster was designed to be seen close up, primarily in daylight hours. By contrast, the billboard, consisting of twenty-four-sheet printed posters or huge painted signs, must be instantly absorbed, often at a great distance, in fast moving traffic. Today, the single-sheet printed poster is encountered most frequently on hoardings and kiosks, in shop windows, bus and subway stops. To a large degree the function of the printed poster has been usurped by the flashing neon signs of the vertical city and the electronically generated designs that animate such great public spaces as Times Square, Piccadilly Circus and Tokyo's Shinjuku district.

Nevertheless, the poster survives as a vehicle to inform and persuade, perhaps because of its essentially topical nature. Unlike many other forms of artistic expression, posters are made in response to specific needs. In his 1924 book, *The Art of the Poster*, the American expatriate designer E. McKnight Kauffer wrote:

The Poster is more strictly commissioned than most other work. Usually the advertiser insists that all essential detail be incorporated in the design and also that the design be such as will appeal to the public. This public has rarely been consulted. It lurks, a vague but hulking shadow, anxiously consulting the Poster for relief from its numberless ailments; it is desperate for food, shivering for lack of clothing, with a mind greedy for books, periodicals and newspapers, and it has a face of its own that should not be ignored; it is indeed, a truth-seeking, nervewracked mass, uncertain and mysterious. This public, which it is the aim of the designer to attract, instinctively is his antagonist and remains such until otherwise proved. The good Poster may be compared to a well-selected fly cast by a skilful [sic] angler who knows his particular fish.

This prescient statement was made long before the advent of Madison Avenue's demographic analyses of the consumer society. While Kauffer's public was a mysterious, undifferentiated mass, it has since become, thanks to these coldly practical studies, a predictable amalgam of specialized audiences whose needs have been clinically charted. No longer does the poster maker address a monolithic audience; market research targets specific segments of the population. There is little risk or mystery left. Indeed, it may be this lack of risk that explains the dearth of individuality and invention in much graphic design today. Images are now too often the product of group thinking, an impersonal process that leads to routine execution and repetition.

Peter Behrens
A.E.G.
1907, lithograph
26⅝ x 20¾, 67.7 x 52.8
Collection Merrill C. Berman

General Electric Company
A.E.G. metal filament lamps
about 1 watt per candle power

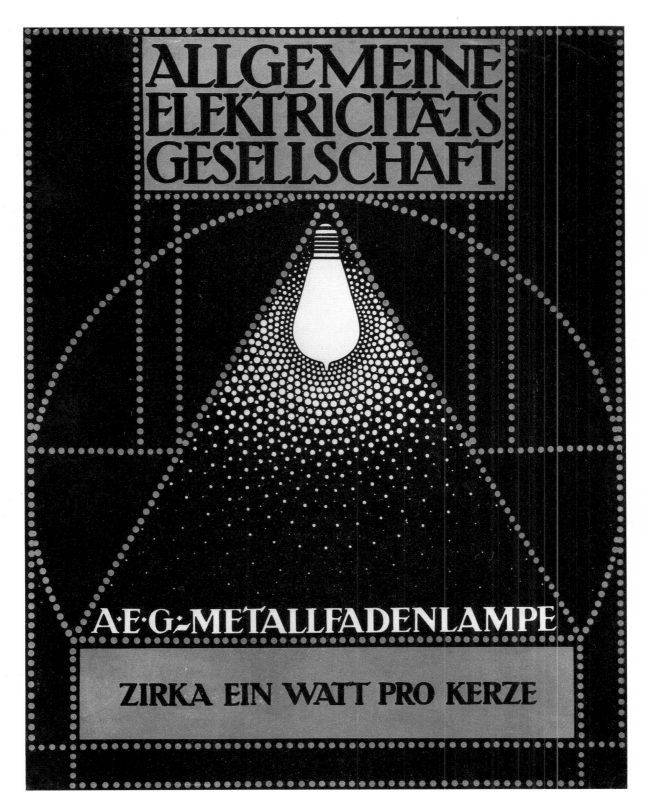

Such was not the case in the innocent early days of poster making. At the turn of the century art and technology came together in fresh, vibrant imagery. A combination of large, flat color areas, vigorous line and minimal text were the poster maker's hallmarks. Not only painters, but such architects as Hector Guimard and Henry van de Velde worked in this vigorous medium. For architects, the poster became a didactic tool to increase public awareness of their design attitudes. They brought their ideas about scale and form to this medium and often carried concepts explored in the three-dimensional world of architecture into print. This transference of three-dimensional form to the flat surface was fully explored in the work of Peter Behrens, the early German modernist, whose association with A.E.G. (General Electric Company) included not only the design of factories and exhibition halls, but on occasion, the graphics that appeared in those spaces. A celebrated Behrens poster of 1907 (p. 9) uses pure geometry to marvelous effect: a simple lightbulb radiates dots in a cone-shaped pattern that throws metaphoric light on the poster's typographic message. Behrens also created an A.E.G. logotype in a beehive-patterned hexagon that was used in print and incised into the brick facade of the company's turbine factory, also designed by Behrens. Environmentalism in its infancy. Other architects of that period, among them the Secessionists Josef Maria Olbrich and Josef Hoffmann, as well as Charles Rennie Mackintosh of the Glasgow School, also concerned themselves with the design of all aspects of a given place—site, building, furniture and graphics—an approach that demands a very strong formal conception.

A similar marriage of visual forms coincided with a resurgence of social concerns in post-World War I Europe and post-Revolutionary Russia. The search for a new social order spawned a number of idealistic movements in politics and in the arts. The rise of the common man required a universal language of symbols expressive of the newly articulated goals of the utopian society. This search led in two directions. The first was toward pictorial modernism in which widely recognized images became the means of communicating with a diverse audience from all walks of life. The Russian icon and the lubok—a broadside using folk imagery—were transmuted into the ROSTA (Russian Telegraphic Agency) window, in which a comic striplike serial imagery was displayed in buildings as a means of reporting and influencing events. The other direction was toward abstraction, and led to the design of easily recognizable visual symbols that conveyed political and social messages.

Through the elimination of elements that were regarded as simply decorative, the idealists of the 1920s hoped to create a universal visual vocabulary of basic geometric forms that did not represent nature but instead was symbolic of ideas. This desire was inherent in such diverse artistic and social philosophies as Dadaism, De Stijl, the Bauhaus and

El Lissitzky
Beat the Whites with the Red
Wedge
1919, lithograph
(n.i.e.)
Collection Stedelijk Van
Abbemuseum
Eindhoven, The Netherlands

[The "red" Bolsheviks fight
against Kerenski's "whites."
Both forces are represented with
the symbols of the new
Constructivism.]

Russian Constructivism. Advocates of the new symbolism searched for forms and techniques appropriate to the new society. The dada poets and painters extracted letters and words from their linguistic context, released letters from language, using them as independent elements, sometimes combining them cinematically with photography. Alexander Rodchenko, a leader in the development of post-Revolutionary Russian art, liked to use photography because it was "fast, cheap and real" and, with many other artists and designers of that era, he took the photograph out of the salon into the daily lives of the people.

As a revolutionary tool the Russian poster attracted a widespread audience. The agitprop (agitational propaganda) train was literally a moving signboard covered with visual messages that brought the aspirations of the Revolution to the countryside. The dynamic geometry of lines, triangles and circles in El Lissitzky's 1919 poster "Beat the Whites with the Red Wedge" could be understood by those who could not decipher the simplest verbal message. In his 1980 history of modern art, *The Shock of the New*, Robert Hughes points out that between 1917 and 1923 over three thousand posters were produced to carry the new political and social ideology to the far reaches of the Soviet Union, an astonishing feat in a country where mass communication had previously been unknown. The same dramatic use of posters is found in China and in many third world nations today.

As E. McKnight Kauffer in his perceptive 1924 book points out:
Symbols convey by imagery what we should otherwise have to ponder over . . . . The symbol becomes . . . the most essential element in present-day design.

Simultaneous with this quest for a universal visual language were efforts to create typefaces that would be expressive of contemporary life. From 1925 to 1928 at the Dessau Bauhaus, Herbert Bayer pursued the goal of absolute legibility in a series of bold, typographic experiments. He created an entirely lowercase alphabet and used it in his posters that were often made up of typography alone, depending upon the design of the letterforms and their relationships within the poster to attract the viewer. In 1928, Jan Tschichold, whose training in calligraphy led him to typography, carried the Bauhaus ideas a step further in his influential treatise, *The New Typography.* In it he advocated the utmost economy of means in design that would be expressive of the modern world. His analysis of type function later led him to the conclusion that appropriateness to content was more important than formal purity, a view that has since been widely adopted by graphic designers.

Like the Russian propagandists, Bauhaus artists wanted their work to be exposed to a broad public. They too created portable exhibition pavilions and sidewalk kiosks; building facades were designed to support posters and gigantic banners. The Polish artist Henryk Berlewi, expressing a view that was shared by many early 20th-century artists, discussed his work in

KUNST GEWERBE MUSEUM ZÜRICH

13. Juni – 30. August 1981

Ausstellungsstrasse 60

Museum für Gestaltung

Schreibkunst.
Schulkunst und Volkskunst in der deutschsprachigen Schweiz 1548 bis 1980

Öffnungszeiten:

Di-Fr	Mi	Sa/So	Montag
10-18 Uhr	10-21 Uhr	10-12, 14-17 Uhr	geschlossen

Druck: Wassermann AG/Basel   DESIGN WEINGART

The 1890s mark the poster's beginning as an active medium for the selling of ideas, the motivation of consumers and the expression of artistic and design ideals. During that decade poster production exploded in concert with the Industrial Revolution, the growth of consumerism and private enterprise, a renaissance in the appreciation of culture, and radical changes in the arts that were both technological and aesthetic. The tendency among many historians who have discussed the posters of this period has been to treat them indiscriminately under the stylistic category of Art Nouveau. Even though the overwhelming majority of that period's posters falls into this category, it is necessary to extract the relatively few but immensely important examples that altered certain characteristics of Art Nouveau to form the earliest foundations of 20th-century design, and to spare them the implication of irrelevancy for the future that was the fate of the Art Nouveau poster in general. In the history of the 20th-century poster these atypical, vital works should be considered as "early modern posters."

To understand the origins that both the typical Art Nouveau and the early modern poster shared, one would need to investigate a myriad of artists, art movements, aestheticians, philosophers, craftsmen and technicians from the Middle Ages to the 1890s itself. Suffice to say here, contemporary poster design in the late 19th century was a fortuitous product of technological developments in color printing and the ferment in 19th-century artistic expression and ideals. A Cook's tour of the period would include a look at such technological developments as the discovery of lithography by Alois Senefelder and Jules Chéret's contributions to color printing in posters; the social and philosophical implications of the anti-naturalistic revolt of Ruskin, Pugin and Owen Jones; and William Morris's involvement with Gothic and medieval ideals that led to his unified approach to all of the arts and crafts and the establishing in England of design guilds, decorative arts museums, and art and design journals. Other significant inclusions would be the artistic influences of William Blake's drawings and illustrations in the early 19th century; the Pre-Raphaelite and symbolist painters' approaches to certain themes and composition; Walter Crane's emphasis on line; the proto-Art Nouveau movement in Great Britain; and, most important, the discovery and importation into Europe of the Japanese woodblock print.

The artistic heights of the Art Nouveau poster had begun to be reached by 1895. By then, almost every major poster artist of the period was producing his best works. Some artists such as Toulouse-Lautrec, Theophile-Alexandre Steinlen, Pierre Bonnard, and Eugene Grasset had several years of poster making behind them; but the list of others who made their first posters in 1894 or 1895 included such significant names as Aubrey Beardsley, the Beggarstaffs, Will Bradley, Georges de Feure, Charles Rennie Mackintosh, Henri Meunier, Alphonse Mucha, and Privat-Livemont. With this burst of activity, a recognizable diversity of styles was clearly seen between the Art Nouveau poster and what can be called the early modern poster, although there were basic design characteristics shared by all of these designers. These were a preoccupation with a swelling and sinuous line, a shallow, almost flat picture plane, a dominance of naturalistic motifs and a striving for a sense of fluid harmony. Yet, the ultimate pioneers of the early modern poster were able to discard, rework, or strongly emphasize certain of these characteristics in order to make their unique stylistic contributions. Art Nouveau poster makers, on the other hand, intensified these characteristics and developed them with a degree of eccentricity and self-indulgence that limited their influence on the future of the poster. This development is best seen in the work of Alphonse Mucha. His posters, and those of his followers, abounded with the classic Art Nouveau iconography of full-figured women with flowing hair who were surrounded by flora and fauna and opulent, architecturelike ornament. The picture area overflowed with detail, and a strong air of mysterious symbolism was evoked. Art Nouveau's linearity was taken to an extreme, as undulating lines crossed each other and bent back upon themselves. As an exponent of the Art Nouveau style, Mucha was the most flamboyant and complex, as he drew upon a wide variety of sources that were both modern and historical, as well as academic and personal.

In extreme contrast to the work of Mucha and his followers are a handful of immensely influential posters by William Nicholson and James Pryde who, to avoid a confusion between their poster making and their painting, called themselves the Beggarstaffs. Their poster images were stripped to bare bones. They employed a minimum of descriptive detail omitting such things as facial features, colors of clothing, or even fingers on hands. Their work was pure outline and broad, flat areas that did little more than suggest the theme of the poster. Even the informative aspect of their posters was kept to a minimum with their harmoniously bold and succinct hand-drawn lettering that was the forerunner of the early 20th-century illustrative-calligraphic German poster. Besides espousing simplicity, the Beggarstaffs seemed to recognize that the poster was a special medium that needed to communicate its message with the greatest possible directness in order to have profound effect. They were led in this direction by Japanese prints of the late 18th and early 19th centuries and by Toulouse-Lautrec, who was also inspired by those amazing works.

The power of the Japanese print lay in its radical flatness, asymmetry and linearity. The Japanese masters were able to depict expression and movement with short, quick strokes, or to use long, continuous gestures to render or imply features of a landscape. But the most important contribution of Japanese prints to Art Nouveau graphics and posters was the use of broad areas of color. This approach led to the characteristic flat color patterning of works by Toulouse-Lautrec, the Beggarstaffs, and others, who later influenced the great German poster designers of the pre-World War I period, such as Lucian Bernhard and Ludwig Hohlwein.

If the last five years of the 19th century represented the Art Nouveau poster at its height, then the first five years of the 20th century saw the modern poster buffeted by artistic crosscurrents. By 1900 Toulouse-Lautrec was dead. Mucha, Steinlen, the Beggarstaffs, Bradley, Penfield and other important poster designers had either stopped or made posters infrequently, while in Italy, poster designers belatedly practiced a version of Art Nouveau based largely on a watered-down heroic Symbolism. In that year, the Germans had yet to launch their major reorganization of the commercial poster—this would begin to take place three years later—but while the commercial poster in this period was stagnating, a new development was slowly taking place in the cultural domain. This was the gradual emergence of the multi-faceted designer, primarily architects and furniture designers who also made posters. Among the most significant were Charles Rennie Mackintosh, Henry van de Velde, Josef Maria Olbrich, Bruno Paul, Josef Hoffmann, Koloman Moser, Alfred Roller, Hector Guimard, and somewhat later on, Peter Behrens. While the total output of each was small in number (from one to a handful of posters), their influence on the 20th-century poster was immense as these architects and designers altered the Art Nouveau poster style. While the essence of this restrained, geometric and severe manifestation of Art Nouveau was at its most concentrated in Glasgow and Vienna from 1894 to 1902, its roots were found as early as the mid-1880s in British crafts and architecture in the work of Christopher Dresser, Arthur Mackmurdo, Charles Voysey and Charles Ashbee. Much of this new form was based on linear approaches that ranged from strict geometry to a leisurely and restrained curvilinearity. As was the case with all stylistic manifestations of Art Nouveau, the early English style also appeared belatedly in posters, specifically in 1894 when three members of the Glasgow School (Herbert McNair, his wife Frances Macdonald and her sister Margaret, who was married to Charles Rennie Mackintosh) designed a large poster for The Glasgow Institute of the Fine Arts. Though this poster has immediately recognizable elements of classic Art Nouveau, such as the floral and stem motifs and the mysterious symbolistlike faces and posturing, its nearly taut lines, graceful curves, the feeling of openness and spaciousness and the overall compositional sense of ornament separate it from flamboyant Art Nouveau.

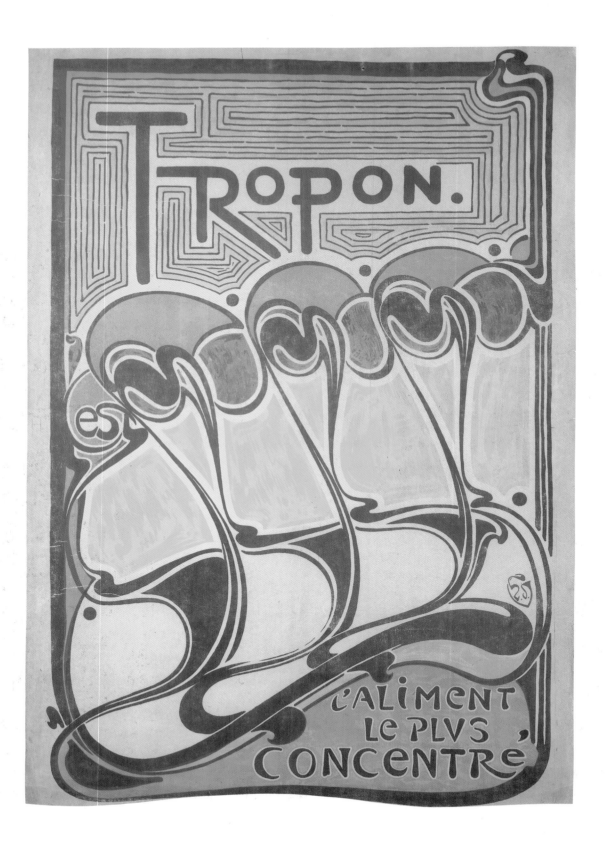

Henry van de Velde
Tropon
1899, lithograph
43⅞ x 30½, 111.5 x 77.5
Courtesy Barry Friedman, Ltd.

Tropon, the most concentrated
food.

Lucian Bernhard
Manoli
1915, lithograph
27¾ x 37¾, 70.6 x 96
Collection Merrill C. Berman

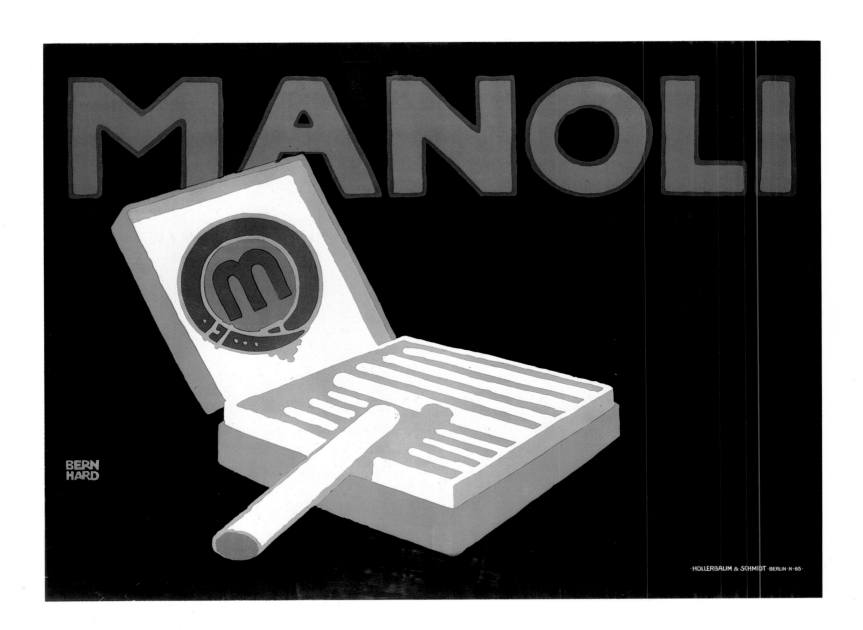

Hector Guimard
Exposition Salon du Figaro le
Castel Béranger
1900, lithograph
(n.i.e.)
Collection The Museum of
Modern Art, New York
Gift of Lillian Nassau

Exhibition The Béranger Castle
Leading meeting house in the
city of Paris.
[a number of details are listed]

Nowhere outside Great Britain was the influence of Mackintosh and modern British design felt more than in Vienna between 1900 and 1903. By then, the Austrian capital had become the center of applied arts in Europe with the establishing of the Vienna Secession in 1897 and the Wiener Werkstätte in 1902. It was the poster that clearly brought together the artists and designers, as in the Secession poster between 1899 and 1902 of Gustav Klimt and the previously mentioned Roller, Moser, Olbrich, and two posters for the Wiener Werkstätte by Josef Hoffmann in 1905. Two Secession posters for exhibitions held consecutively in 1902 show the Viennese poster style at its height. While both are transitional examples of design, there are interesting differences between them. In Koloman Moser's poster for the XIII Secession Exhibition, an allegiance to Mackintosh and his group, most particularly the Glasgow Institute poster, is clearly evident. Both posters involve the same general design strategy based on deliberate elongation of the body as contrasted to the head, the treatment of facial characteristics as abstractions, and the making of the body beneath the head as near-solid form. Moser, however, has substituted a circle over the heads for a similarly placed oval in the Glasgow poster and further geometrized the total composition, including the lettering. The end result is the reinterpretation of the Mackintosh poster as an exercise in geometry instead of fantasy. Roller's composition for the XIV Secession Exhibition stands in stark contrast to the Moser poster, even though both are extreme examples of the ornamental poster. Here Roller used geometry to build up patterns to create an anti-naturalistic approach to the design. While Roller refers to Art Nouveau by using flat surfaces, some linear motifs, and the *de rigeur* female nude, the continuous, omnipresent flowing line associated with the style has been forsaken for an extreme and dramatic breaking up of the surface that, when later filtered through Cubism, reappeared in both cultural and commercial posters of the 1920s.

While the influence of British and Viennese artists and designers played the central role in the development of the cultural poster inthe early 20th century, there are two significant posters derived from the more flowing French and Belgian Art Nouveau that cannot be overlooked in this context. Both were done, in 1900, by architect-designers: the Frenchman Hector Guimard and the Belgian Henry van de Velde. Although Guimard's "Exposition Salon du Figaro le Castel Béranger" was not the only poster made up exclusively of lettering in the Art Nouveau style, it was the only truly great one. It has a transcendental monumentality that one rarely encounters until the era of the post-World War I avant-garde. The letter-forms are of the style and period, but they are designed and arranged to express a new sense of dynamism and rationality. This is achieved by varying the color and size of the letters and by the almost imperceptible ornamentation that appears in the background. Furthermore, the "Castel Béranger" poster, without the use of illustration, captures the essence (much as a classic Bauhaus poster) of the total artistic style that was Art Nouveau.

At first glance, the "Tropon" poster (p. 18) of Henry van de Velde appears to be a totally abstract design in an aggressive Art Nouveau style. Yet this poster has a realistic subject which has never before, as far as we know, been noted. Tropon, as the message implies, is a nutrient made from egg whites. In the poster, the artist has represented the whites of the eggs being separated from the yolks. This startling, pioneering use of highly-abstract imagery to make an indirect allusion to something concrete makes the "Tropon" poster a conceptual forerunner of the avant-garde posters of the 1920s. These later images were often concrete and abstract at the same time, even if the design was stylistically very different.

In the decade between 1895 and 1906, the history of poster art changed from an intriguing, exotic, historical and often introspective style, to one that marked the beginnings of the rational, functional, dynamic and eclectic approaches to modern design. Perhaps most significantly, the dichotomy between the illustrator as commercial poster maker and the artist-designer-architect as cultural poster maker became more clearly defined. In the former group, Lucian Bernhard revolutionized commercial posters with his 1903 design for Priester matches, in which two matchsticks were depicted against a brown background with just the single word "Priester." As a disciple of the Beggarstaffs, Bernhard inspired a whole group of other poster designers, including Ludwig Hohlwein. Together, Bernhard and Hohlwein, in somewhat differing ways, turned the commercial poster from the "function follows form" aesthetic of the typical Art Nouveau poster to one in which the product (in the case of Bernhard) or the appropriate setting or mood (Hohlwein) became the determining factor. Their emphasis on clarity, simplicity and visual "legibility" not only characterized German product posters, but became the predominant poster making style in Switzerland. Illustrators in these two countries were by far the most important creators of commercial posters from 1905 to 1920.

The period from 1906 until 1910 saw a slowing of activity by architects and designers in the poster form. With the exception of Hoffmann's posters in 1905 for the Wiener Werkstätte and Peter Behrens's 1907 classic for the A.E.G.—both of which strongly anticipated Bauhaus functionalism—and a small number of interesting lettering and ornamentally abstract posters by relatively unknown graphic designers, the greatest posters of the 1908 to 1910 period were significant for their contribution to the body of German and Austrian Expressionism. These posters were quite idiosyncratic and did not lead to a new direction in the cultural poster. It would not be until the post-war period ten years later that Cubism, Dadaism, photomontage, Russian Constructivism and Italian Futurism would show the way to a second "Golden Age" of poster design.

Robert Brown is co-owner of the Reinhold-Brown Gallery, New York, which specializes in fine and rare poster art from the early decades of this century.

In 1936 Alfred Barr opened his book *Cubism and Abstract Art* with a comparison of two posters (p. 24). Both were produced to advertise the 1928 international exhibition of printing held in Cologne. Barr's purpose was to draw attention to the contrast between the "fairly realistic poster style common to mediocre travel posters the world over," of the one, and the "simplicity and abstraction" of the other.[1] Here, the "natural objects are reduced to flat, almost geometric forms arranged on a strongly diagonal axis under the influence of Russian Suprematism." The reason that two different posters were produced was that they were intended for different markets—one for the Anglo-American, "accustomed to an over-crowded and banally realistic style," the other for the German public, which, "through the activity of its museums and progressive commercial artists was quite used to an abstract style." For Barr, the superiority of the formal, abstract poster was self-evident. He ends his comment by saying "Today, times have changed. The style of the abstract poster, which is just beginning to interest our American advertiser is now discouraged in Germany." Later in the book he comments on the political cause of this discouragement, the rise of National Socialism.[2]

Certain assumptions in Barr's pictorial preface are worth spelling out. First, the status of the poster: it is treated not as a secondary art but as an art form in its own right, like painting, photography, theater, film. In his catalogue of the exhibition that the book accompanied he lists the category as "typography and posters." Second, there is the implication that, while the simplicity of the abstract poster was good in itself, it was particularly

1. Alfred Barr, *Cubism and Abstract Art* (New York: The Museum of Modern Art, 1936). Barr's book accompanied the first major historical survey exhibition of modern movements in art.
2. Barr discusses the contradictory ways in which abstract art became involved in politics, with, for example, the Nazis suppressing abstract art and International Style architecture while fascist Italy welcomed them. A footnote was added, as the book was going to press, on the refusal of U.S. customs to allow in, as art, nineteen pieces of sculpture that were to be in the exhibition, because they did not represent a human or animal: "This essay and exhibition might well be dedicated to those painters of squares and circles . . . who have suffered at the hands of philistines with political power."

(p. 22)
Alexander Deineka
Transforming Moscow
1931, lithograph in two parts
(left) 40¾ x 28½, 103.7 x 72.4
(right) 41¼ x 28⅜, 104.8 x 72.2
Collection Merrill C. Berman

Transforming Moscow into a
model socialist city of the
proletarian state.

Nöckur
Poster for the Pressa, Cologne
1928
(n.i.e.)

[World Press Exhibition]

Ehmcke
Poster for the Pressa, Cologne
1928
(n.i.e.)

good in a poster where the need for simplicity had long been recognized as intrinsic. The question might arise as to whether an abstract poster is necessarily simpler than a figurative one—look at the radical simplifications of the Beggarstaffs, for example. The difference here is that the simplicity of Barr's poster is based upon abstract geometrical principles independent of the subject depicted, and the complex of ideas underlying Barr's prejudice will be examined in detail later. He implies that the more abstract design is more functionally effective than the other. Because the result of the abstraction in this case is to focus attention on the typography, it is of course especially apt, given that the poster is advertising an exhibition of modern printing. But Barr would clearly favor an abstract design whatever was being advertised. When he uses the term "abstraction" in this case, he does not in fact mean total non-figuration. Although it is doubtful whether an Anglo-American audience would recognize in the triangular shapes a "reduction" or "abstraction" of Cologne cathedral's twin towers, the fact remains that these geometrical shapes retain an element of figuration, however reduced, which has the function of keeping them distinct from the typography. But many posters in the 20s and 30s did use totally non-figurative designs. Does this mean that the poster image as distinct from its typography ceased to function? In other words, that in so far as it was abstract it became simply an adjunct to the typographical message?

I would like to look at the question of function and abstraction in poster design in the first three decades of this century, and to consider the ways in which the main movements within modernism influenced and absorbed the poster, and reciprocally to what extent they fed off it. To focus on these questions and narrow my argument to those posters directly or indirectly connected with modernism and its roots is, obviously, to look at only a tiny fraction of the total poster production of this period. Whole areas have to be excluded, including historical and political events that spawned innumerable poster campaigns such as the two World Wars. However, the inquiry will necessarily involve sociopolitical and historical issues given the interdependence of the poster and society. Why, for example, was the Anglo-American market, as Barr describes it, resistant to or ignorant of abstract design? What contributed to its success in Europe? Barr's optimism about the arrival of an abstract style in American advertising was to be short-lived. World War II brought to an abrupt end experimental graphic design and before the war, in Germany, the Nazis had condemned modern typography and returned to black letter gothic. On both sides, Axis and Allies alike, a conservative realism (which had of course always coexisted) swept across the entire field of poster production and more or less eliminated the abstract-constructivist style. It is, incidentally, a significant comment on the divided nature of poster studies that the literature on World War II posters often entirely ignores this remarkable fact, leaving out the way a poster looks altogether. Although the poster has its own history and

A juxtaposition of these illustrations of English hoardings of 1844 (top) and 1900 demonstrates the growing sophistication of advertising methods at the turn of the century. The placement of duplicate posters in series is an important example of the development of visual communications techniques in this period.

conditions, it tends to be treated in different ways according to the discipline involved: as an illustration of social or political history, as an aspect of the history of marketing and advertising, as a branch of art and design.

The poster had, during the period I want to discuss, a spectacular energy, and this energy has never really been recovered since World War II. Its conditions had changed for good. The poster belongs to a specific phase in the age of mechanical reproduction: for seventy or eighty years it was the most conspicuous, accessible and familiar form of pictorial production. After the First World War it was joined by the film and the illustrated weekly paper, which had, in El Lissitzky's opinion, triumphed over the easel picture. "The invention of easel pictures produced great works of art, but their effectiveness has been lost. The cinema and the illustrated weekly magazine have triumphed."[3] For a while the poster was the ally and support of the cinema. But it was eventually displaced by television, and now, in Europe and the United States at least, its function has been taken over by print advertising.[4]

Almost from the beginning of poster history there have been the poster and the art poster. Before the 1870s, and excluding special categories like the recruiting poster, the vast majority of advertisements in public places took the form of words. A few woodcut posters included pictures, but usually with the accompaniment of a long text. Primarily it was easily printed slogans and the titles of plays, books and products that were plastered over the walls. Before the regulation of hoardings began it was virtually a war, too, to see who could get his poster on top. A comparison was drawn in an article in *The Poster* in 1900 between a hoarding of 1844 and one at the turn of the century. This was intended to show the improvement of the regulated order of the contemporary hoarding with its practice of "blocking" or placing groups of a single poster together. Although this photograph still shows a preponderance of the typographical poster, the pictorial poster was by this time very well established. The potential of the colored lithograph for posters had been recognized in the 1870s. Some of the earliest examples were enlarged versions of book illustrations hung up in bookshop windows to advertise new publications. It was in the late 1860s that Jules Chéret brought together his technical experience as an apprentice lithographer in England and the lesson of the Japanese color woodblock print with its bold shapes and flat washes of brilliant color, which had been a powerful influence on impressionist and post-impressionist painting in Paris, to create the conditions for the poster boom in the 80s and 90s. This is often described in poster histories as the

3. "Our book" (1926), in Sophie Lissitzky-Küppers, *El Lissitzky* (London: Thames and Hudson, 1968), p. 361.
4. In the case of the firm of Guinness, which still mounts extensive poster campaigns on well-placed hoardings, the ratio of money spent on advertising is four to one in favor of film, which they find the most cost effective way of reaching their target audience.

HARPER'S
is the largest and most popular **MAGAZINE** yet owing to its enormous sale and in spite of the great expense of production, the price is

STILL

ONE SHILLING

The Artistic Supply Co. Ltd.
Amberley House W.C.

Printed by Stafford & Co, Netherfield, Nottm   Copyrighted in America, 1895.

Beggarstaffs

The Beggarstaffs
Harper's
1895, lithograph
86⅜ x 78¼, 219.5 x 198.5
Courtesy Reinhold-Brown
Gallery

"golden age" of the poster, and with nostalgic exaggeration as the highest point reached by the poster before or since. Many of these posters were publicity for books, theater and cabaret—much the same subjects as those on the 1844 hoardings. This was the area dominated by the artist-poster designer: Chéret, Henri de Toulouse-Lautrec, Alphonse Mucha (Sarah Bernhardt's preferred artist), Félix Vallotton. Such posters were almost immediately collectors' items, with price lists and catalogues, and they were frequently stripped from the walls by enthusiasts before the paste was dry. But commercial manufacturers were also quick to recognize the value of the lithographic picture poster, especially for products like food, drink or soap. By 1900 some were even using the new photographic halftone process for the image. Most such posters, though, were designed by printers, either on speculation or on commission from an advertising agency or directly from a company. The fact that artists were seldom involved was due less to the prejudice of the artist than to the prejudice of the manufacturer. The artist was not trusted to make a comprehensible and desirable image. When Henry Davray was asked by the Paris dealer Deschamps to organize an exhibition of English posters he succeeded in scraping together a few by Aubrey Beardsley, the Beggarstaffs and Maurice Grieffenhagen, but he found a constant complaint by the artists that they were hampered by the advertisers' insistence that the "tin of cocoa or shoe polish, brand of soap or cigarettes" should be shown in its external packaging, which seldom had anything very aesthetic about it.[5] The Beggarstaffs' radical designs, that sometimes used large cutout paper shapes and drew, as did Lautrec and Chéret, on the flat colors and silhouettes of the Japanese print, were unpopular, and were even satirized as grim and gloomy. The generally conservative attitudes of the manufacturers persisted after the war in England and the United States, though more daring publicity came to be associated with such products as tires and cars.

The distinction between the poster and the art poster (the *plakat als solches* as opposed to the *kunstlerische plakat* as the German magazine *Das Plakat* defined it in 1914) was not necessarily between the function of advertising an aesthetic as opposed to a consumer product, but was rather a reference to the status of the designer. But for such reasons as I have outlined above the term art poster was most frequently used for those concerned with cultural as opposed to commercial interests. Within this, there were posters with a specific relationship to an art movement and which therefore acted as a visual manifesto, as aesthetic propaganda, clearly displaying their status as art. Good examples of this would be the posters produced in association with the Secession in Vienna and Germany. In Glasgow, the Macdonald sisters and Herbert McNair designed an

5. *XIXth-Century French Posters*, with an introduction by James Laver and a preface by Henry Davray (London: Nicholson & Watson, 1944).

exhibition poster for The Glasgow Institute of the Fine Arts, which shares with the Viennese posters the highly decorative features of the pervasive Jugendstil. Within this decorative ideal the poster's specific function is realized: it is not a question of simply reproducing a representative work of art and adding some lettering. Stress is laid on the design as a whole, with close attention to the typography which is often highly stylized, complementing the emphatic linearity of the image. Sometimes it is adapted to fit around the image, or given a separate box, and in some cases becomes the major element in the design. The stylization of the letters sometimes leads to distortion and internal inconsistency, and even within a poster the same letter may be shaped differently (the length of the central stroke of the E varies, for example, in McNair's poster). Such lettering was to be condemned as idiosyncratic and random when the call for standardization came in the first decade of the 20th century.

The art poster dominated the field leading up to the turn of the century. It was a time when poster magazines and societies flourished, and hoardings were proliferating through town and country. Posters had become a pervasive pictorial presence, and as such drew strong responses from artists and critics. Ruskin, a reluctant witness to the massive growth of poster advertising, expressed the view that it would finally usurp painting: "The fresco painting of the bill sticker is likely, so far as I see, to become the principal fine art of modern Europe: here, at all events, it is now the principal source of street effect. Giotto's time is past . . . but the bill poster succeeds," he wrote from Florence in 1872.[6] The poster, at certain times and for different reasons, has represented the condition to which painting itself would aspire. "Be a poster: advertise and project a new world," was the call to a new generation of constructivist artists in the Prague review *Disk* in 1923. This represents an extreme position which was part of a complex of ideas I shall return to.

At the beginning of the machine age the poster was "a piece of modern furniture that painters immediately knew how to use."[7] A street aesthetic had begun to replace the "secular idealism" of the earlier 19th century, magnetizing those who wanted art to remain in close contact with life. "We would at any price reenter into life," the futurist painters wrote in their 1910 *Technical Manifesto*.[8] Apollinaire, critic and champion of the cubists, and an admirer of the futurists, included scraps of overheard street conversations in his poems, and located art outside its conventional lairs—the salon, museum, or review:

You read prospectuses catalogues posters singing out loud
There's poetry for this morning . . .[9]

The fauve painters included brilliantly colored poster hoardings in their works, and Robert Delaunay used poster signs and images as essential elements in his simultaneous visions of city life. Fernand Léger, in his writings, developed the notion that the true source of visual ideas lay in the world of industry and technology. In the Paris Fair, at the annual Aeronautical and Automobile Salons, a new kind of beauty was to be found which put to shame the "vast, dull, gray surfaces, stuck in pretentious frames," of the paintings in the Salon d'Automne.[10]

I am amazed to see that all those men who arranged the splendid display boards, astonishing fountains of letters and light, powerful or precious machines . . . don't understand or appreciate that they are the real artists, that they have upended every modern plastic idea.[11]

It was not a matter, for Léger, of taking this modern spectacular as a subject, but of learning from it new pictorial principles. The most essential of these was contrast, and for this the poster provided the most vivid example.

This yellow or red poster, shouting in a timid landscape, is the best of possible reasons for the new painting; it topples the whole sentimental literary concept and announces the advent of pictorial contrast.[12]

El Lissitzky described how Léger's postwar, post-cubist painting had achieved its ideal:

With the new canvas . . . the culture of painting no longer comes from the museum. It comes from the picture gallery of our modern streets—the riot and exaggeration of colors on the lithographic poster . . .[13]

The futurist leader Marinetti celebrated the new industrial age in his "The Founding and Manifesto of Futurism": *We will sing of the great crowds excited by work, by pleasure and by riot; we will sing of the multicolored polyphonic tides of revolution in the modern capitals; we will sing of the vibrant nightly fervor of arsenals and shipyards blazing with violent electric moons; greedy railway stations that devour smoke-plumed serpents . . .[14]*

Both Léger and Marinetti used the poster as a sign of the industrial world as opposed to the country. "Multi-colored billboards on the green of the fields, iron bridges that chain hills together, surgical trains that pierce the blue belly of the mountains . . . " Marinetti wrote in "War, the World's Only Hygiene."[15] The violent clash between billboard and natural landscape

6. John Ruskin, *Fors Clavigera. Letters to the Workmen and Labourers of Great Britain* (Index, etc. [Compiled by the Rev. J. P. Founthorpe] 9 vol., Orpington: G. Allen, 1871–1887).

7. *Functions of Painting,* ed. and introduction by Edward F. Fry, with an article by Fernand Léger, "Contemporary Achievements in Painting" (London: Thames and Hudson, 1973).

8. Gleizes and Metzinger, "Cubism" (1912) from Robert L. Herbert, *Modern Artists on Art* (Englewood Cliffs, New Jersey: Prentice-Hall, 1964), p. 3.

9. Guillaume Apollinaire, "Zone" (1912), from *Alcools, Poems, 1898–1913* (Paris: 1913).

10. Fernand Léger, "The Machine Aesthetic, the Manufactured Object, the Artisan and the Artist" from *Léger and Purist Paris* (London: Tate Gallery, 1971).

11. Ibid.

12. "Contemporary Achievements in Painting," op. cit., p. 12.

13. El Lissitzky, "Exhibitions in Berlin" (*Veshch* 3 Berlin, 1922), Sophie Lissitzky-Küppers, op. cit., p. 346.

14. F. T. Marinetti, "The Founding and Manifesto of Futurism" (*Le Figaro,* 20 Feb. 1909), ed. U. Apollonio, *Futurist Manifestos* (London: Thames and Hudson, 1973).

15. F. T. Marinetti, "War, the World's Only Hygiene," ed. A. Mondadori, *Teoria e Invenzione Futurista,* 1968, p. 261.

is also a symbolic opposition between past and present, the harmonious rural scene and the modern industrial street. The image of the brilliant hard-edged poster slicing into the "sentimental" landscape does of course belong to a period before the spread of advertising was strictly controlled, when it was far more invasive and striking both in town and country than it is today. Ruskin grumbled about the spread of advertisements for "prayers and wares," and was particularly distressed by the religious posters plastered all over the facade of one of the most beautiful churches in Florence, " . . . in and out upon the sculptured bearings of the shields of the old Florentine knights."[16] Léger, by contrast, was outraged by attempts to control the spread of billboards, a characteristic failure, as he saw it, of the so-called "men of good taste" to recognize the pressing if brutal demands of the new state of things. He links it to the general failure of the public to understand modern art.

It has even given rise to a stupefying and ridiculous organization that pompously calls itself 'The Society for the Protection of the Landscape.' Can anyone imagine anything more comic than this high court of worthy men charged with solemnly decreeing that such and such a thing is appropriate in the landscape and another thing is not? By this reckoning it would be preferable to do away with telegraph poles and houses immediately and leave only trees, sweet harmonies of trees . . . . There is nothing worse than habit, and you will find the same people who protest with conviction in front of the billboard writhing with laughter at the Salon des Indépendants in front of modern pictures, which they are incapable of swallowing . . .[17]

While Léger sought to emulate the effect of the poster in its environment, abstracted from its function, Wyndham Lewis, the English vorticist writer and painter, imagined annexing it to serve directly as aesthetic propaganda. Lewis, who, like the futurists, was fully alive to the possibilities of mobilizing the new means of mass communication for his own purposes, envisaged the poster as a means of converting the public to abstract art:

Let us give a direct example of how this revolution will work in popular ways. In poster advertisement by far the most important point is a telling design. Were the walls of London carpeted with abstractions rather than the present mass of work that falls between two stools, the design usually weakened to explain some point, the effect architects rally would be much better, and the public taste would thus be educated in a popular way to appreciate the essentials of design better than picture galleries have ever done.[18]

The poster had pushed its way into the consciousness of painters like Léger and Delaunay. It made an appearance in a much less direct way in the difficult, esoteric Cubism of Picasso and Braque. When lettering was smuggled onto late analytic cubist canvases, hovering ghostlike on the surface and often the only immediately "legible" element on it, posters, like newspapers or bottle labels, could have been the occasion for it. In Braque's

Le Portugais of 1911, the stenciled letters refer to a poster for a ball, and serve to locate the man as sitting at a café table, the poster on the glass wall of the café or glimpsed through it.

But none of these painters was interested in poster design for its own sake, and neither Cubism, nor Futurism, had a direct impact upon it. Cubism, of course, through its crucial influence on a number of artists who traveled through it on a road to abstraction (like Mondrian, or Malevich), was strongly to affect postwar art, architecture and design. Cubism itself always remained an art of realism though, and when Mondrian or Malevich developed their abstract or non-representational art it was founded upon a different set of ideas.

There is almost no evidence of a geometrizing abstraction which could be ascribed to the workings of a cubist influence in poster design until the middle of the First World War, to judge by the most important poster magazine of the time, *Das Plakat*. *Das Plakat* was published in Berlin from 1909 until 1921, its internationalism barely ruffled by the war. It covered most aspects of the poster, with theoretical articles as well as a quantity of excellent reproductions of posters from all over Europe and from the United States, including commercial, political and cultural ones. It is therefore a valuable guide to the state of the poster during this period. The Munich designer Ludwig Hohlwein was generally recognized as the dominant figure before (and indeed during) the war, and *Das Plakat* devoted its May 1913 issue to him. His work can be compared to the flattened and simplified style of the Beggarstaffs. Like them, he placed a heavy emphasis on silhouette, but while Pryde and Nicholson kept a strong linear element that bounded or complemented the large flat areas of color, Hohlwein almost eliminated it. The formalized shapes composing the figures are defined usually by contrast with a neighboring tone or hue; he often used a negative-positive contrast, and sometimes the effect is curiously like a painting from a halftone print. His elegant silhouetted figures were well adapted to the clothing advertisements that formed a major part of his prewar output.

Not until June 1916 is there a hint of Cubism of any kind. In that issue of *Das Plakat* an article was published entitled "Cubism and the Poster" by a Dr. Wolf. He goes straight to the heart of Cubism with works by Picasso, both analytic paintings and collage, rather than by followers like Albert Gleizes and Jean Metzinger. The posters reproduced for comparison can only be called cubistic. The most interesting example is by Oskar

16. Ruskin, op. cit.
17. Fernand Léger, "Contemporary Achievements in Painting," op. cit., p. 12. Much later, Léger recalled the dramatic intervention of posters in the landscape: "The streets, the countryside, those impressionist landscapes, which were so melodic and pleasant, have suddenly seen "Dubonnet" signs appearing everywhere: the melody got all fucked up—there is no other word . . ." "La couleur dans l'architecture" (1954) in Fernand Léger, *Functions of Painting*, op. cit., p. 185.
18. Wyndham Lewis, introduction to vorticist exhibition, Doré Gallery, London, 1911.

LEIBNIZ-AKADEMIE

DAS

3

TRIADISCHE

BALLETT

BURGER
HÖTZEL SCHLEMMER

VORVERKAUF BEI KETTNER GEORGSTR 34
UND I.D. LEIBNIZAKADEMIE GOETHESTR 2^A

SCHAUBURG: DIENSTAG 19. FEBRUAR 8 UHR
DIENSTAG 26. FEBRUAR 8 ABDS.

DRUCK: REINECK & KLEIN WEIMAR

Oskar Schlemmer
Das Triadische Ballett
1921, lithograph
32⅛ x 22⅛, 81.5 x 56.2
Collection Merrill C. Berman

The Triadic Ballet
Leibniz Academy
Dancers: Burger and Hotzel
[dates, place, ticket sales are
listed]

Schlemmer, in which a head is reduced to flat black and white geometric forms, prophetic of later developments but least like cubist painting as it existed at the time.

Das Plakat picked up dada, reproducing a Raoul Hausmann "poster" in 1920, but not De Stijl. In 1920 it also published a number of Soviet posters, but these did not include examples of suprematist or constructivist designs.

When I mentioned the "simplification" of Secessionist posters above, I was not referring to cubist simplification, but rather to a quite independent influence on design in the prewar years: the German Werkbund. The Werkbund was founded by Hermann Muthesius in 1907 with the aim of improving the standards of German design and encouraging and facilitating contacts between industry and designers. It can be seen as having established certain ideas and practices that were to remain of importance after the war, in such contexts as the Bauhaus. It established architecture as the leader in the fields of design, and placed an emphasis on standardization with simplicity, clarity and rationality as primary objectives. This led to direct conflict with Jugendstil, and such figures as Henry van de Velde, who opposed Muthesius in "a spirited rearguard action by an outgoing type of designer."[19] It is interesting to compare posters by van de Velde and Guimard, with posters by Peter Behrens, who was the most complete example of the Werkbund designer. Van de Velde's posters for the food company Tropon (p. 18) use highly stylized organic shapes, reminiscent of Guimard's Paris Metro entrances, which here contrast with the linear pattern surrounding the letters and governed by them in a rather random and arbitrary way. This is an inventive and effective poster, but Jugendstil typography did not place a high premium on legibility. There are Secession posters, and those by the Glasgow "Four," whose lettering holds a fine balance between ornament and clarity, but still could not be referred to as standardized. In Guimard's own poster it reaches an unprecedented degree of illegibility.

The Werkbund designers moved toward a simplicity governed by rational order. Behrens had joined the A.E.G. in 1907 as design consultant for all A.E.G. products (buildings, manufactured objects and publicity). Initially a painter and graphic designer, he continued to produce posters after becoming an architect, as well as designing lamps, teapots and a sewing machine. His 1907 poster for A.E.G. uses an architectural motif, but no longer as a separate image. It has become a framework for the design as a whole. The lightness of the later poster is related to a change in Behrens's own architectural practice, in that he moved from solid, heavy

19. Reyner Banham, *Theory and Design in the First Machine Age* (London: The Architectural Press, [1960] 1975), p. 78.

factory buildings to structures conceived of as envelopes over a vast industrial space. But Behrens is not here reproducing a glazed and abstracted neoclassical industrial temple, but reworking his industrial aesthetic in terms appropriate to the function of the poster. Muthesius had stressed that attention to function was to govern the search for formal solutions to problems of mechanical production. In his speech to the 1911 Werkbund Congress, whose theme was "The Spiritualization of German Production," he "introduced the idea of standardization as a virtue, and of abstract form as the basis of the aesthetics of product design."[20] Although he did not apparently have in mind the abstract geometry of mathematical proportions, the ideas are remarkably similar to the neo-platonic, post-cubist Paris movement, Purism, which was founded in 1918 by Amédée Ozenfant, and by Charles Edouard Jeanneret (Le Corbusier), who had attended this Congress as a young architect. Purism proposed the selection of manufactured objects based upon pure geometric shapes as subjects for painting. To return to Behrens's poster, there is perhaps an incipient abstract geometry in the forms—the rectangular arch, the incomplete arc of a circle, the triangle of the lamp's rays—but they are not conceived of as primarily abstract forms independent of the object in the way that Suprematism, De Stijl and Constructivism were to do. The type of radical simplicity of Behrens's design, growing out of but rejecting the decorative abstractions of the Arts and Crafts movement, exemplifies the theory and practice of a movement concerned with industrial design in the broadest sense. It was not, in other words, the result of imposing new pictorial ideas onto the field of graphic design.

Three movements began during World War I that were to influence, in various ways, graphic design: Suprematism in Russia, De Stijl in Holland and Dadaism in Zurich (and subsequently all over Europe). Dada inherited the futurists' publicity methods, flooding the newspapers with stories (or fables), the public with leaflets and the art world with exhibitions and reviews, but it rejected their positive celebration of the machine aesthetic and glorification of war. Dada engaged in a wholesale rejection of society, its art and its war, that involved it immediately in a contradiction. Most of its (not very numerous) members were writers or artists, most living off the production of words and images. Dada's well-publicized nihilism, though, has often been allowed to mask its positive side. There was no identifiable dada "style:" dada includes the sophisticated ironies of Duchamp, the satirical anti-militaristic graphics and photomontages of John Heartfield and George Grosz, the abstractions of Jean Arp. But certain ideas and methods were held in common. The irrational was valued in a world where sense and rationality had led to or at least been powerless to stop the "civilized carnage" of war.[21] One method of bypassing controlling reason was chance. Feeding into experiments with chance were ideas culled from Eastern philosophies which recognized that the flux or chaos of nature was a salutary and necessary reminder to man of his place within rather than above it. Another dada method was to force a return to pre-cultural forms: to reduce language to its basic components of sound or letter, or to emulate children's drawing. At the other end of the scale was parody: futurist simultaneity, cubist collage, were subjected to various degrees of subversion. Dada also refused the conventional medium of oil paint, and its search for new materials, ready-made or found or simply previously unthought of as art, was to reverberate on through the 20th century.

Dada differed greatly in the various centers where it was active. In Zurich, where it began in 1916, dada artists took "abstraction as the cornerstone of their new wisdom."[22] Marcel Janco, the Rumanian artist, who at this time was making abstract reliefs in plaster and wood, made two posters for the second dada season in Zurich in 1917. One was for the first dada exhibition at the Galerie Corray in January (p. 37), the other was for the second *Sturm* exhibition and featured a drawing by Janco of primitive sculpture. The earlier poster was, like many dada works, composed entirely of lettering. The framework of the repeated "dada," characteristic of the obsessive self-publicity of the movement, is written in childishly uneven capitals, as though chalked on a blackboard. This is deliberate and significant, representing the "primitiveness, beginning again at zero" that dada stood for.[23] As Hugo Ball said, "childhood as a new world; all the directness of childhood, all its symbolic and fantastic aspects, against the senilities of the adult world."[24] "Dada" curling round in unbroken repetition is also reminiscent of dada sound poetry. Hugo Ball read his first sound poems in Zurich in 1916, and although these did not reach the pure phoneticism of Hausmann's or Kurt Schwitters's later work, he felt he had "developed the plasticity of the word to a point which can hardly be surpassed."[25]

Dada in Berlin differed radically from dada elsewhere. Conditions were more extreme: starvation, defeat, revolution, made this one wing of dada actively political. Much of Berlin dada took on the aspect of street art. The montages by Grosz and Heartfield, mixing graphic elements, cut up or complete photographs and scraps of printed text, anticipate the use of montage in posters later in the 1920s. Many of them were made for the satirical magazines put out by Wieland Herzfelde in Berlin just after the war, during the period of the abortive German revolution and the establishment of the Weimar Republic. In these the technique of photomontage was first systematically exploited for political ends. Many works looked like posters

20. Ibid., p. 72.
21. Hugo Ball, *Flight Out of Time: A Dada Diary* (June 1916) (New York: Viking Press, 1974), p. 67.
22. Richard Huelsenbeck, "En Avant Dada: A History of Dadaism" (1920), in Robert Motherwell, *Dada Painters and Poets* (New York: Wittenborn, 1951), p. 37.
23. Richard Huelsenbeck, "Dada Lives!" (1936), Motherwell, op. cit., p. 280.
24. Ball, op. cit., August 1916.
25. Ibid., June 1916.

and even functioned as such. At the Berlin Dada Fair of 1920, poster placards were stuck among the works, which were themselves hung not only all over the walls but often on top of one another, so that the whole wall looks like a hoarding. The works were hung, in other words, not to facilitate individual contemplation and spiritual immersion, like a conventional exhibition, but to arrest, buttonhole, shock and amuse the public. Individually and collectively, in a sense, they were aiming at the condition of a poster. Hausmann printed his phonetic poems such as FMBSW on large sheets of colored paper. Made to be declaimed, in giving them typographical form, Hausmann made them preeminently visual. One slogan at the exhibition read: "Art is dead—long live the machine art of Tatlin," witness to the curiosity and affinity Berlin dada felt for the as yet largely unknown art of the new Soviet Republic, and also heralding the complete relationship that was to take place between Dadaism and Constructivism after the war.

The typographical experiments, casually revolutionary, that characterize so many dada productions, began with the third issue of Tristan Tzara's Zurich periodical, *Dada*. On the cover there is overprinting, and the lines are arranged at odd angles, disrupting our conventional reading habits from left to right, in a horizontal line. *Dada* was produced on a minute budget, Tzara paying for most of it himself with Jean Arp and Janco subsidizing four more pages. They went to an anarchist printer, Julius Heuberger, and appear to have selected the typefaces and played freely with the layout themselves.[26] Tzara's "Salon Dada" poster (p. 125), made for the exhibition during the 1921 dada season in Paris, harks back typographically to his poem "Bulletin" in *Dada 3*, in which each line was printed in a different font. Any sequential sense the poem might have had is destroyed by the sloganlike distinctness of each line. In the 1921 poster this is taken to a logical extreme, with each separate announcement, either practical or apparently quite irrelevant, literally framed to become a sign on a signboard. In the lettering for the title of the exhibition, Tzara mixed both typefaces and upper and lowercase letters on a random basis, contradicting all accepted typographical manners.

There were, of course, precedents for dada's typographical experiments. One that could really be seen as falling within dada itself was an advertisement in the Berlin magazine *Neue Jugend,* for a Grosz portfolio, that scatters words and images freely across the page. There was a long tradition of adapting the printing of a poem to add a counterpointing visual dimension to the page, of which Apollinaire's *Calligrammes* was one of the most recent examples. The futurists made spirited attacks on the rigidity of

26. Dada did not discriminate in its choice of typefaces; old-fashioned and modern examples were used equally, with the occasional addition of letters from decorative alphabets. They could not afford the expense of such special printing as Marinetti's *Parole in Libertà,* nor were they sufficiently interested technically to take their involvement as far as the compositor.

Marcel Janco
1.Exposition.Dada
1917, woodblock
16⅝ x 10⅜, 42.3 x 26.3
Collection Elaine Lustig Cohen

First Dada Exhibition
Cubists-Negro Art
Conference on art made by
Tristan Tzara

Kurt Schwitters, Theo van
Doesburg
Kleine Dada Soirée
1923, lithograph
11⅞ x 11¾, 30.2 x 29.9
Courtesy Ex Libris

Kurt Schwitters
Merz = von Kurt Schwitters
1923, lithograph
18⅛ x 23, 46.2 x 58.5
Collection Merrill C. Berman

Expurg[ated]
by Kurt Schwitters

Read the journal *Merz*
Editorial office Hanover

Woman delights with her legs
I'm a man, I don't
have any [picture of a cherry]
Kurt Schwitters

MERZ=

von KURT SCHWITTERS

ANNA BLUME

O du, Geliebte meiner siebenundzwanzig Sinne, ich
liebe dir! — Du deiner dich dir, ich dir, du mir.
— Wir?
Das gehört (beiläufig) nicht hierher.
Wer bist du, ungezähltes Frauenzimmer? Du bist
— bist du? — Die Leute sagen, du wärest, — laß
sie sagen, sie wissen nicht, wie der Kirchturm steht.
Du trägst den Hut auf deinen Füßen und wanderst
auf die Hände, auf den Händen wanderst du.
Hallo, deine roten Kleider, in weiße Falten zersägt.
Rot liebe ich Anna Blume, rot liebe ich dir! — Du
deiner dich dir, ich dir, du mir. — Wir?
Das gehört (beiläufig) in die kalte Glut.
Rote Blume, rote Anna Blume, wie sagen die Leute?
Preisfrage: 1.) Anna Blume hat ein Vogel.
2.) Anna Blume ist rot.
3.) Welche Farbe hat der Vogel.
Blau ist die Farbe deines gelben Haares.
Rot ist das Girren deines grünen Vogels.
Du schlichtes Mädchen im Alltagskleid, du liebes
grünes Tier, ich liebe dir! — Du deiner dich dir, ich
dir, du mir, — Wir?
Das gehört (beiläufig) in die Glutenkiste.
Anna Blume! Anna, a-n-n-a, ich träufle deinen
Namen. Dein Name tropft wie weiches Rindertalg.
Weißt du es, Anna, weißt du es schon?
Man kann dich auch von hinten lesen, und du, du
Herrlichste von allen, du bist von hinten wie von
vorne: „a-n-n-a".
Rindertalg träufelt streicheln über meinen Rücken.
Anna Blume, du tropfes Tier, ich liebe dir!
KURT SCHWITTERS

DAS WEIB ENTZÜCKT DURCH SEINE BEINE
ICH BIN EIN MANN, ICH HABE KEINE.
KURT SCHWITTERS

KIRSCHBILD   KURT SCHWITTERS

LESEN SIE DIE ZEITSCHRIFT MERZ. REDAKTION HANNOVER, WALDHAUSENSTRASSE 5

the printed word. Poems were printed to make their appearance parallel their sound, so that a crescendo in volume was indicated with an increase in the size of the letters. Futurist poems of this kind were printed in the first dada review in Zurich, *Cabaret Voltaire,* of June 1916. Marinetti, in his manifesto "Wireless Imagination and Words in Liberty" of 1913 challenged the whole notion of syntax, and was equally rude about the "decorative precious aesthetic of Mallarmé," who, in *Un Coup de Dés*, had his poem printed so that any natural reading order was destroyed. Marinetti wanted "a swift, brutal and immediate lyricism" which could only be achieved in print by attacking the typographical harmony of the page. "On the same page, therefore, we will use *three or four colors of ink,* or even twenty different typefaces if necessary. For example: italics for a series of similar or soft sensations, boldface for violent onomatopoeias." When his "Words in Liberty" was published in 1919 visual effect exceeded his earlier ideas. But even the liberation of futurist printed poetry seems systematic beside the anarchic typographical vagaries of many dada posters and reviews. The point is that there was no dada system, but it is not so easy as it may seem to act or construct without any system. At their most interesting, dada works have allowed the material to be explored or simply to exist for its own sake— including typography. The notion of "direct" creation led dadaists to a position close to the formalist and anti-art theories of Russian Constructivism, and prepared the way for collaborations such as those between Kurt Schwitters and El Lissitzky.

Delaunay's abstract design for "soirée du coeur à barbe," (p. 124), which took place on 6 July 1923, is an oddity. By this late date in the history of dada the quarrels and intrigues between dadaists and between dada and the avant-garde had reached baroque proportions. Suffice it to say that it was now Tzara's turn, though for different reasons, to enter into suspect collaboration, in this case, in the interests of keeping dada alive in Paris. He put on an evening entertainment of poetry, music and theater with the help of Jean Cocteau (a particular bête noire of dada), Zdanevitch, and a group of Russians involved in avant-garde theater: Tcherez. Zdanevitch ran a Université faculté russe—41°, which met in a café on the Boulevard Montparnasse, and whose name was intended to reveal its "creative fever" (p. 125).[27] Tcherez had been putting on literary cabarets in a spirit close to dada and was its natural ally, but Breton and his Littérature group felt there was enough provocation to justify them in physically disrupting the performance. Breton was expelled by the police, and, as (semi) organized activity, dada in France was over; the surrealist option held the field. Delaunay's involvement was in fact less "suspect" than it appears. He figures quite frequently on the fringes of dada activity, as participant and as object of attack. A bold spirit, happy to engage in public action, he never modified his painting through any dada ideas. The previous year, in May 1922, Breton had approached Delaunay to make posters for a demonstration he and a few friends were planning, to go on sandwich boards that they would wear. Delaunay, he felt sure, would like nothing better than to join in himself.

Dada had, and still has, a long tailpiece. Marcel Duchamp, for one, continued to design posters, catalogues and book covers that could often be described as dada inventions. Sometimes they comment ironically on the historicizing tendency of the event they publicize or commemorate. A 1953 poster (p. 178) for example, whose layout was designed by Duchamp, was, when sold or sent through the post, to be, following Duchamp's instructions, crumpled into a ball. "This could account," as Richard Hamilton commented, "for its comparative rarity."[28]

De Stijl, unlike dada, was founded on a positive set of theories. It was an international movement, which started in 1917 in Holland with the publication of the review *De Stijl,* edited by Theo van Doesburg, with, initially, the close support of the painters Piet Mondrian and Bart van der Leck. De Stijl was to become a major theoretical and practical force in graphic design, painting and architecture after the war. Its main theoretical underpinning in the first few years was provided by Mondrian, who defined his concept of Neoplasticism in the first issue as follows:

This new plastic idea will ignore the particulars of appearance, that is to say, natural form and color. On the contrary, it should find its expression in the abstraction of form and color, that is to say, in the straight line and clearly defined primary color.

When this was written, Mondrian was still in the process of realizing this ideal in practice, and was working in close contact with Bart van der Leck. In 1916 van der Leck had moved to Laren, near Amsterdam, where Mondrian had already settled. He had been working as a designer for the firm of Müller & Co. in The Hague since 1914, producing publicity, and also color schemes for interior design. The Batavier-Lijn poster (p. 42) already shows a schematic, geometrical reduction of the objects and figures, which look ancient Egyptian, placed horizontally to the picture plane to eliminate perspective. It is interesting to compare this with his *Study for Composition 1917 no. 5 (Donkey Riders)* (p. 42). In the final version the riders and donkeys are abstracted to a series of blue, red, yellow and black rectangles of regular width on a plain ground. The influence of Mondrian's "plus and minus" works of 1915–16 was apparent in the two-dimensional linear patterning in earlier stages of the composition, but van der Leck's use of colored rectangles seems in turn to have encouraged Mondrian to experiment with free-floating color planes. It is significant, however, that when Mondrian began to paint following van der Leck's example, as in *Composition in Color*

27. Michel Sanouillet, *Dada à Paris* (Paris: 1965), p. 301.

28. Arts Council of Great Britain, *The Almost Complete Works of Marcel Duchamp*, exh. cat., 1966, Tate Gallery.

Bart van der Leck
*Study for Composition 1917
no. 5* (*Donkey Riders*)
1917, gouache on paper
(n.i.e.)
Courtesy J. P. Smid,
Kunsthandel Monet

Bart van der Leck
Batavier-Lijn
1916, lithograph
28½ x 42⅞, 72.1 x 108.5
Collection Merrill C. Berman

Batavia Line
Cheapest and fastest route
Regular service for freight and
passengers

A of 1917, he did so in terms of purely pictorial elements, with no reference to subject matter. In his plus and minus compositions a synthesis was being enacted which had, as its terms, both the earlier church facade and pier and ocean series. In other words, whereas van der Leck had worked progressively towards abstraction from a particular point of reference (van Doesburg followed a similar process in his progressive abstractions, *The Cow*) Mondrian was striving for a universal basis for his abstraction. Both van der Leck and Mondrian now eliminated any residual reference to subject matter, but Mondrian was unhappy with the random appearance of the color planes in his canvases, and commented, "While working I discovered that the color planes against a flat ground do not create a unity for my work. In van der Leck's work it seems to be possible, but he works in a totally different way."[29] To retain unity, a concept central to his theory of Neoplasticism, Mondrian began, in 1919, to anchor his color planes to a grid of black or gray vertical and horizontal lines, striving to retain the flatness of the actual canvas in the composition. In van der Leck's completely abstract canvases he, unlike Mondrian, introduced diagonals, cutting the edges of his rectangles. The effect of these compositions was, as Mondrian noted, one of balance and unity. This could be ascribed to van der Leck's greater decorative instinct, or what might be described as an attraction to symmetrical patterning and repetition. For Mondrian, on the contrary, unity had to be the result of a balance of *opposites.* For him, the vertical and horizontal, for example, stood for such opposing qualities as male and female, spiritual and earthly, tragic and harmonious, and the final asymmetric composition was to resolve the tension between them.

Whereas for Mondrian the introduction of the particular would destroy the abstract and therefore the universality of his painting, it was relatively easy for van der Leck to adapt his painting once again to the depiction of specific objects—as in the "Plantennet Delfia" poster (p. 98) where the color planes are arranged to compose the image of a bottle. Van der Leck was always an idiosyncratic figure within De Stijl and in some ways these posters are not representative of the movement. The overwhelming De Stijl influence in graphic design was the use of strong vertical and horizontal lines and rectangles, either as typographical markers or as the arrangement of the text, or as independent abstract elements.

De Stijl was dedicated to the creation of new forms appropriate to modern man whose life, Mondrian said, "was becoming more and more a-b-s-t-r-a-c-t."[30] Its concerns were not primarily functional; it believed that art should serve as a "model for future life."[31] Although there was a

29. Letter to Bremmer, early 1918, cited in Rudolf W. Oxenaar, "Van der Leck and De Stijl, 1916–1920," in *De Stijl: 1917–1931, Visions of Utopia* (New York, Minneapolis: Abbeville Press, Walker Art Center, 1982), p. 69.

30. Piet Mondrian, "De Nieuse Beeldung in de Schilderkunst," *De Stijl*, I, 1, Oct. 1917.
31. Hans L. C. Jaffé, "Introduction," in *De Stijl: 1917–1931*, op. cit., p. 11.

dogmatism within De Stijl (Mondrian for example finally resigned from it when van Doesburg introduced diagonals into his painting), the magazine itself, under van Doesburg's editorship, was both polemical and highly receptive to new ideas.

Posters were a comparatively incidental aspect of De Stijl activity, but it did maintain a lively interest in typography. Van der Leck, in his posters, fragmented his letters, stencil fashion, to parallel his fragmented planar images, but not according to any strict geometry. The lettering on Huszar's title page for the first issue of *De Stijl* is also divided into single components, here regularly geometrical, but in the interests of matching the purely abstract woodcut design rather than creating a standardized typography. Indeed, they match the image so well that they read first as shapes and only secondarily as letters. This was quite deliberate; as Huszar said, his intention was to "give black and white equal value, without ground," an aim hardly compatible with legible lettering.[32] Huszar continued to experiment with figure-ground egality, and in the 1929 poster for the exhibition of contemporary industrial arts it has become a positive, rather obstructive element through the introduction of a color contrast (p. 46). There were various experiments with geometrical letterforms in the 1920s which showed scant regard for legibility. Piet Zwart, for example, designed logos based on the square, rectangle and circle. There is, of course, a difference between a logo and a poster, and the distortion of the logo is much modified in the poster lettering, as can be seen in the ITF poster (p. 47). Van Doesburg devised a basic uppercase alphabet in 1918–19, whose proportions could be altered and exaggerated at will vertically or horizontally (e.g., his "Section d'Or" poster, 1920). Beside the basic alphabets designed at the Bauhaus in the 20s this looks curiously mannered. Van Doesburg did not use this alphabet exclusively, but alternated happily between dada and a more austere constructivist typography. In the 20s new features, such as the diagonal, entered De Stijl design, which will be discussed below in the context of international Constructivism.

In both dada and De Stijl, posters as such were relatively peripheral. They did exemplify a general typographical curiosity, or a dominant visual aesthetic, but they were produced according to local or specific demands. In Russia, from 1917, the poster was to have a crucial social and political role, and to become central to the theory and practice of a group of revolutionary artists who came to be known as constructivists.[33] The poster held a peculiarly prominent position in Russia following the Revolution, during the Civil War and blockade, and then in the years of reconstruction. It had first of all an enormous educational and propaganda function. The need for pictures was vital in the task of reeducating the people in the aims and ideals of the new communist state. "During the civil war and blockade, pictures outstripped and often replaced the press, the megaphone installed in a public square or the eloquence of the orator at mass meetings."[34]

Not only did they transcend the language barrier in a land with a multinational population, but they overrode the barrier of illiteracy, a gigantic problem in the construction of a new state seventy-five percent of whose people were unschooled. In the early days of agitprop the task was to transform as many visible surfaces of buildings, ships and trains as possible. Huge panels hid the neoclassical facades of buildings, trains were painted with slogans and pictures of stock caricature figures designed to give a simple and immediately graspable message. Street posters, like illustrated newspapers, were there both to be looked at and, by those who could, read.

Our younger generation of artists accumulated much latent energy during the 1917 Revolution, energy which only needed big demands on the part of the people to reveal itself. The audience was the mass of the people, the great mass of semi-literates. The Revolution has carried out colossal propagandist and educational work. The traditional book was, one might say, divided into separate pages, enlarged a hundredfold, painted in brighter colors and hung up in the street as posters. Unlike the American poster ours was not planned to be taken in at a single glance from the window of a passing car, it was meant to be read and digested at close range . . .[35]

Many of the posters, such as those El Lissitzky describes above, were intricate and beautifully colored. Often woodcuts, they treat the Revolution symbolically (a peasant ploughing with a sunrise behind him and the czarist crown and jewels trampled into the ground), for instance. Many were before and after scenes of the life of the peasant and the landowner, and they sometimes took the form of an illustrated story with a series of pictures and texts. There was no tradition of the political poster in Russia, although the

32. Cited in Kees Broos, "From De Stijl to a New Typography," *De Stijl: 1917–1931,* op. cit., p. 147.

33. The term "Constructivism" is not identical with any single movement or group of artists, nor is it easily susceptible to a single definition. "Constructive" or "constructivist" came into general use by avant-garde critics and artists after the First World War, to explain new artistic practices in which representation was no longer a concern. In sculpture, traditional methods like carving and modeling were rejected in favor of building or constructing form out of planes, volumes and lines. There was stress on the use of new materials and on the study of material for its own sake. Many of the ideas are derived from Cubism and Futurism (in sculpture). The term can be associated with "abstract," but the two are by no means interchangeable. In the USSR between 1920 and 1924 artists calling themselves constructivists could hold different and even contradictory views. In Europe, *De Stijl* was a major forum for constructivist ideas in all branches of the plastic arts and in architecture. In 1922 the Congress of Constructivist Artists at Weimar included constructivists and dadaists such as Jean Arp, Kurt Schwitters, Theo van Doesburg, Hans Richter, Cornelis van Eesteren and El Lissitzky. El Lissitzky's role in spreading Russian Constructivism in Europe was vital, but the more purely abstract Constructivism of Naum Gabo was more influential in England and the United States.

34. Szymon Bojko, *New Graphic Design in Revolutionary Russia* (London: Lund Humphries, 1972), p. 32.

35. El Lissitzky, "Our Book" (1926), Sophie Lissitzky-Küppers, op. cit., p. 358.

ET

AA
B·N·A
K·V·B·
VANK
25
JAAR

1999

TENTOONSTELLING

VAN HEDENDAAGSCHE
KUNSTNYVERHEID
KLEINPLASTIEK
ARCHITECTUUR

STEDELYK MUSEUM
AMSTERDAM
29·JUNI — 28·JULI
GEOPEND VAN 10·5
INGERICHT DOOR DEN TENTOONSTELLINGS
RAAD VOOR BOUWKUNST EN VERWANTE KUNSTEN

V. HUSZAR

Vilmos Huszar
Tentoonstelling van
Hedendaagsche
Kunstnyverheid, Kleinplastiek,
Architectuur
1929, lithograph
27½ x 23½, 69.9 x 59.7
Collection Merrill C. Berman

Exhibition of Present Day
Artifacts
Plastic Art, Architecture
City Museum of Amsterdam
[dates and other details are
listed]

Piet Zwart
ITF
1928, lithograph
42⅞ x 30⅝, 108.8 x 77.8
Collection Merrill C. Berman

An international exhibition in
the film domain
[dates, place, times are listed]

Kasimir Malevich
What have you done for the front?
1919, lithograph
(n.i.e.)

bloody satirical graphics and cartoons of the 1905 Revolution were a source for the agitprop posters. The major source was the printed broadside or lubok (a term referring either to the limewood block from which it was printed or the baskets from which it was hawked). By the mid-17th century large numbers of these were being sold. They were often couched in religious symbols, and there was also a tradition of the broadside icon. There were traditional stories and legends, but also picture stories with specific local and historical significance. The lubok is characterized by a deliberately crude stroke, flat color washes and a clear composition, and many of the early agitprop posters, such as those of the poet Vladimir Mayakovsky, are clearly modeled on this popular street imagery (p. 121). An arsenal of stock caricatures was built up, designed to give simple and easily graspable messages: fat landowner, false priest, heroic peasant and soldier. They reflect the fact, too, that the vast majority of the population worked the land; industry was not to become a subject or object of poster campaigns immediately.

Besides this natural extension of street culture, artists of many different tendencies mobilized to help, including the most advanced artists who had been developing radical nonobjective art under the last years of the czarist regime. They, severally, believed they had a peculiar right to determine what art appropriate to a revolutionary society should be, including its street propaganda. The suprematists in particular flung themselves enthusiastically into the task, harnessing their abstract designs (not always successfully) to the demands of street and theater demonstrations. A May Day parade in Vitebsk was transformed by Malevich and his pupils: "The red brick of the main street is covered here with white paint. Green circles, orange squares and blue rectangles swarm over this white background."[36] Lissitzky, who had been working with Kasimir Malevich, and Malevich himself, produced posters for the recruiting campaign on behalf of the Red Army fighting for the Bolshevik government against the White Russian threat in the Civil War. Both are examples of the pure abstract geometrical forms of Suprematism pressed into service for agitational purposes. In Malevich's poster for a ROSTA window, "What have you done for the front?," the slogan is surrounded by suprematist "elements" shooting out from the curved and shaded surface of, presumably, the globe. Malevich had enthusiastically welcomed the Revolution, but saw no need to adapt his commitment to a visionary abstraction in the interests of a specific message: "Innovators of the whole world, a new pole of the revolutionary axis is forcing our heavy sphere to turn," he wrote, and it is this vision that his poster is intended to convey.[37] In Lissitzky's poster "Beat the Whites with the Red Wedge" (p. 11) the suprematist forms of the circle, triangle and rectangle, still based on Malevich's original source forms of 1915, are given symbolic functions, easily recognizable within the framework of the campaign: red wedge for the Red Army (whose uniform included a red star on the helmet) and white for the counter-Revolutionary forces. But how recognizable would this poster have been? Would the message have been perceived as clearly as that in the famous British recruiting poster by Alfred Leete, "Your Country Needs YOU"? Did Lissitzky's poster, if lacking in specific clarity, have a more universal inspirational quality? These questions were to be raised in theoretical terms again and again as artists became increasingly absorbed in the problem of function.

The genesis of the ROSTA window-poster campaign was described by Victor Shklovsky:

Denikin's (Commander of the White Army during the Civil War) offensive was under way. It was imperative that the streets should not be silent. The shop windows were blank and empty. They should bulge with ideas. The first window of satire was set up in Tverskaya Street in August 1919. A month later, Mayakovsky began working.

Before Mayakovsky, each window was a random collection of drawings and captions. Each drawing was a separate unit. Mayakovsky introduced central ideas: a whole series of drawings connected by a rhymed text that went from picture to picture . . .[38]

Mayakovsky and his collaborators worked together in cold and cramped conditions: "Mayakovsky made the posters, the others prepared stencils by cutting out cardboard according to a design; still others used the stencils to make copies." ROSTA continued to publish propaganda and information posters until 1922.

Neither Lenin nor Trotsky sympathized with the claims of the advanced artists on the left, but under Lunacharsky, the head of the People's Commissariat of Enlightenment, in charge of both cultural and educational policy, they were encouraged with state patronage, and given posts in art schools, and within IZO (Department of Visual Arts of Narkompros).

The futurists, as the avant-garde in general was still termed, immediately after the Revolution, responded energetically to it, and in 1918 published "Decree No. 1 on the Democratization of the Arts," attributed by Szymon Bojko to Mayakovsky. This is an interesting document, marking an early stage in the complex debate concerning the new role of the artist:

1. From today, with the abolition of the czarist regime, the existence of art is suppressed in the warehouses and hangars of the human spirit: palaces, galleries, salons, libraries, theaters.

2. In the name of the great march toward the equality of all in the face of culture, may the Free Word *of the creative personality be seen at the*

36. S. Eisenstein, "Notes about V. V. Mayakovsky," in Zhadova, *Malevich: Suprematism and Revolution in Russian Art, 1910–1930* (London: Thames and Hudson, 1982), p. 32.
37. K. Malevich, "To Innovators of the Entire Universe," (1919) from ed. Olga Makhroff and Stanislas Zadora, *Art et Poésie Russes 1900–1930, Textes Choisis* (Paris: Centre Georges Pompidou, 1979), p. 126.
38. Victor Shklovsky, *Mayakovsky and His Circle* (London: Pluto Press, 1974).

crossroads, the walls of houses, palisades, roofs, the streets of our towns and our villages, on the backs of cars, carts, tramways and on the clothes of all citizens.

3. May pictures (colors) be hung from house to house, in the streets and on the squares, in rainbows of precious stones, rejoicing, ennobling the eye (the taste) of the passerby . . . .[39]

It is clear that the pictures the writer had in mind are not propaganda but art, and the democratization called for is to serve the double function of freeing the artist from his restrictive conventional audience (to allow the free play of his "creative personality") and of bringing art within the reach of all, so that "everyone, coming out into the street, will be enlarged and enriched by the contemplation of beauty." Bojko quotes a passage from this to illustrate how the early agitprop activities intended to "instill a communist awareness in broad segments of society," but this is not primarily what the writer had in mind.[40] The emphasis on collective is already there; what would have grated in particular on participants in the later stages of the debate, as it sharpened, was the emphasis on "creation" and "beauty." As early as 1919, Osip Brik, the critic and fellow employee with the poet Mayakovsky of IZO, launched an attack on definitions of the artist that depended upon these concepts. Brik argues that, indissolubly welded as they are to bourgeois culture, if they are removed there are those who fear that art itself would go along with them, but that in fact there are other artists who "know how to paint pictures and decors, they know how to paint ceilings and walls, they know how to make drawings, posters, signs, they know how to erect monuments . . . these artists have their place in the commune. They execute definite and socially useful tasks . . . ."[41]

It was not part of Brik's purpose to discuss what form these pictures, posters, murals and monuments should take, but over the next two or three years the debate within Inkhuk and Vkhutemas became increasingly concerned with this question.[42] The next step was taken in November 1921, when the Production Group—twenty-five artists, including Rodchenko, Stepanova, the Stenbergs, Gustav Klutsis under the guidance of Brik, Boris Arvatov and Nikolai Tarabukin—withdrew from all theoretical activity. This led to a radical revision of the term Constructivism:

Constructivism is socially utilitarian. Its application is situated either in industrial production (engineer-constructor) or in propaganda (constructor-designer of posters, logos, etc.). Constructivism is revolutionary not only in its words but in acts. It is revolutionary by the very orientation of its artistic methods.[43]

The following phase of the constructivists' struggle to impose their views on the visionary ideology of revolutionary society is in some ways the most extraordinary. It must be clear by now that there were groups of artists going under the name constructivist who held very different and even opposing views, and this was equally true of postwar Constructivism in

Europe. The Production Group, far from abandoning its researches into pure form and material, sought to adapt them to the production of specific objects. As Liubov Popova said, "[We must] find the paths and methods that lead away from the dead impasse of depictive art and advance through knowledge of technological production to a method of creating objects of industrial production, products of organized, material design." Those last three words are significant because they imply a whole series of attitudes to the design of objects which we can define as "constructive." Nothing fortuitous, nothing uncalculated, as Alexei Gan said in his book on Constructivism. Gan himself made posters and worked on the design of his own book; he worked with the compositor on the type and layout (p. 144).[44] The difference between the productivists and constructivists, like Gabo who were influential in bringing the movement to the West was that they eschewed the making of easel painting and sculpture altogether.

The abstract experiments of the previous years were now applied. There is a close relationship between Klutsis's constructivist designs of 1920–1922, which, like similar constructions by the Stenberg brothers, do not even have the role of a "model," however utopian, and his designs for kiosks for the Fourth Comintern Congress (Congress of the Communist International). These obviously had a practical destination, though only two were built, but at the same time they were utilizing the "laboratory" period principles of using material according to its natural properties, eliminating all superfluous detail or ornament, emphasizing the linear as opposed to the

39. "Decree No. 1 on the Democratization of the Arts" (*Gaseta Foutouristov,* 15 March 1918), *Art et Poésie Russes,* op. cit., p. 107.

40. Bojko, op. cit., p. 32.

41. Osip Brik, "The Artist and the Commune, The Artists' Effort," from *Art et Poésie,* op. cit., p. 121.

42. Vkhutemas (Higher State Art-Technical Studios) established in 1920, replaced the Moscow Free Schools, which had been the amalgamation in 1918 of the Moscow School and the Stroganov School. It was geared toward design and in these faculties the constructivists were prominent. The painting faculty was more traditional, and by 1925 had adopted the realism of the AKhRR artists into its curriculum. Inkhuk was a group originally founded by Wassily Kandinsky in May 1920, devoted to theory and research. Many of its members taught in Vkhutemas, and it became a center of constructivist theory.

43. Arvatov, "Two Groups" (1922), cited in M. Rowell and A. Rudenstine, *Art of the Avant-Garde in Russia: Selections from the George Costakis Collection,* exh. cat. (New York: Guggenheim Museum, 1981), p. 226 ff.

44. It was not a matter of rejecting the abstract "laboratory" period of Constructivism except in so far as it was "laboratory," but of utilizing the research into material of that period in conjunction with industrial processes. "A proletarian artist receives an order for a poster. What should he do to make it effective? To make it correspond to the place where it will be hung (e.g., on the surface of a wall), to the spectators to whom it will be shown, to the distance from which they will look at it, to the subject that will be depicted on it (if the poster is figurative), to the ideological influence for which it is intended, etc.? All this can be accomplished on one condition: that the artist knows how to make free use of those materials that go to make up the poster as an expressive and actively organized form; and, moreover, not to use them—as was done previously—in one definite direction (in such and such a 'style'), but in any way, as a given concrete occasion dictates. Inevitably this command of material presupposed an abstract laboratory . . . ." Arvatov, "The Proletariat and Leftist Art" (1922), in Bowlt, *Russian Art of the Avant-Garde: Theory and Criticism 1902–1934* (New York: Viking Press, 1976), p. 228.

Alexei Gan
Twenty years of Works by
Vladimir Mayakovsky
circa 1930, lithograph
25⅝ x 17¾, 65 x 45.1
Collection Merrill C. Berman

[An exhibition held at the
Literary Museum of the Lenin
Public Library, and the Society
for the Furtherance of the
Literary Museum, in 1930, on
the anniversary celebrating

twenty years of work by
Mayakovsky. Following the
closing of the exhibition
Mayakovsky turned it over to the
State Literary Museum where,
during the 1930s, the exhibition
was permanently on view.]

Alexander Rodchenko
Kino-Eye
1924, lithograph
36½ x 27½, 92.7 x 69.9
Study Collection The Museum
of Modern Art, New York
Gift of Jay Leyda

Director: Dziga Vertov
Cameraman: Mikhail Kaufman
Product of Goskino

Alexander Rodchenko
The Press is Our Weapon
1923, lithograph
(n.i.e.)

Gustav Klutsis
Design for a kiosk
1922, linoleum cut
(n.i.e.)
Collection George Costakis

mass in space. They were to be made of wood, rope and canvas and painted red, white and black: red with its now well-established symbolic connection with the new communist state, black and white because they were symbolically constructive rather than decorative. It may be argued that they represented an ideal of utility, economy and efficiency, though they were not necessarily more economical or efficient than other forms might be.

Several of Klutsis's kiosk designs were intended as display stands for posters, and the question now arises—what were the posters to be produced by the "constructor-designers" to look like? It is significant that Klutsis in his drawings for these kiosks represents the posters in position simply with typography. Many of the constructivists' posters at the time (for circus and theater, for example) did rely almost entirely for their effect upon a bold use of the Cyrillic alphabet simplified to maximize its geometrical effect. Occasionally formal abstract elements are introduced subordinate to the words and acting as punctuation marks or directional signs. It is not always obvious whether these are descended from Suprematism or are ingenious uses of the printer's black line. If posters needed images, though, how were they to be reintroduced? People outside the constructivist group were simply continuing the early agitprop style of the ROSTA posters for shop windows. But for Alexander Rodchenko, who was teaching on the "artistic" side of the metalwork faculty while an engineer taught the technical side, there was no obvious solution to this problem. He was, at the time, producing advertisements and book and poster designs for various state institutions, in line with his productivist beliefs, and he made a variety of different experiments in returning to the image.

One of his first designs is a horn of plenty effect, an advertisement for the GUM department store which appeared in *Izvestya* in 1923. It shows a number of isolated objects which could have come straight out of the small ads page of an illustrated Victorian newspaper. By contrast, his poster, "The Press is Our Weapon," slightly later the same year, clearly has in mind Klutsis's kiosk designs, and strikingly adapts formalist design to the image of papers rolling off the presses. It could be argued that the reason for the difference in design was that one was intended for small-scale consumption in the pages of a newspaper, the other for the street. However, I don't think this accounts for the radical difference between the types of images. Uncertain of his direction Rodchenko worked closely with Mayakovsky, who produced the text for the posters and advertisements, and to a certain extent Mayakovsky's own poster drawings, with their simplified, cheerful flat figures and objects influenced him. But Rodchenko's designs are always rationalized to the nearest complete geometrical form—circle, rectangle, square—as in the famous Baby's Dummy advertisement (p. 54). Another device Rodchenko borrowed from 19th-century advertisements was the use of the object advertised as a constructive element in the whole design. These could be fortuitous similarities, and should not be overemphasized,

Alexander Rodchenko
Baby's Dummy
1923, lithograph
(copy by Vladimir Mayakovsky)
(n.i.e.)

because one of the key positions the constructivists held was that culture had to find new forms and methods for the new proletarian society. "We will fight with all our power against the transfer of dead methods of work to today's new art," announced the first editorial in *LEF* (Left Front of the Arts). Their stress on the ideological soundness of constructivist method (which sometimes involved a deliberate ambiguity in the use of the term "materialist") was important because it was in opposition to the Bolshevist leaders' attitude to the bourgeois past: Lenin had no time for the leftists and believed, "We must take the entire culture that capitalism left behind and build socialism with it. We must take all its science, technology, knowledge and art. Without these we shall be unable to build communist society."[45] In 1922 a new body of artists was formed, the Association of Artists of Revolutionary Russia (AKhRR), who promoted a return to a "realist" style, based on the Wanderers group of artists of the 19th century, with workers in new industries, Red Army soldiers and scenes from the recent heroic past as subject matter.

The magazine *LEF* was produced at least in part to stiffen and unify the opposition to what the left artists considered a regressive move. This opposition, it seems to me, was posited in a particularly acute form in the medium of posters, book illustration and advertisements, because there the question of an image comes into play. How is reality to be pictured without slipping back into 19th-century modes? One important solution was found by Rodchenko in photography and photomontage. An unsigned article was published in *LEF* in 1924, called "Photomontage," in which two arguments are put forward stressing the essential difference between photography and conventional pictorial representation.

The combination of photographs replaces the composition of graphic representations. . . . The meaning of this substitution lies in the fact that the photograph is not the sketch of a visual fact, but its precise fixing . . . . A poster about hunger with photographs of the starving produced a much stronger impression than a poster using ordinary sketches of the starving . . .

The second argument presents the technique of photomontage from a constructivist point of view—it has its own proper qualities which are not simply an echo of painting: "Photography has its own possibilities of montage which have nothing to do with the composition of paintings." It goes on to cite Rodchenko's photomontages for Mayakovsky's poem "Pro Eto," and, in the West, the photomontages of Grosz and the other dadaists.

The combination of photography, usually in the form of montaged photographs with formal constructivist design, became the basis for poster design in the hands of Rodchenko, the Stenberg brothers, Klutsis and Prusakov. A major client was Sovkino, established to administer the newly nationalized film industry. Many of the films made under its auspices were documentary, with the function of educating the people in the aims of Soviet society and glorifying the achievements of the state in the reorganization of agriculture and industry.

The film poster, though extraordinarily influential, was not the dominant manner of poster design in the 1920s. The ROSTA windows continued in an early agitprop style, while others reflected an AKhRR attitude with their use of a bloodless realism. One of the most interesting artists who also designed posters was Alexander Deineka. He belonged to a younger generation, and had trained at Vkhutemas from 1921 to 1924 in the painting faculty, where the constructivist influence, which dominated in the basic division and the metalworking faculty, was at a minimum. However, while advocating a return to easel painting with a proletarian subject matter, he avoided a return to the 19th-century Wanderer style. In posters such as "Transforming Moscow" (p. 22), of 1931, he utilizes formalist devices to a much greater degree than in his paintings—the flat geometrization of certain areas is at odds with the Proun-like diagonal tilt of the buildings illustrated on the right half of the poster. Deineka's works are closely involved with Stalin's emphasis on industrialization as the means by which socialism would be brought about in Russia, and the consequent lessening of communist internationalism in favor of nationalism. Although Deineka was criticized in the 30s for his formalism, he was eventually decorated as a Hero of Socialist Labor and was made a full member of the USSR Academy of Arts.

Toward the end of the 20s a new conflict arose between the right and left over photography. Rodchenko was accused of abusing the descriptive, documentary and informative value of a photograph because of the strange angles from which he chose to photograph things. The two children in his *Kino-Eye* poster (p. 52) gazing upwards, exemplify Rodchenko's belief that:

In photography there are old points of view, for example the angle of vision, the view of a person standing on the ground looking straight ahead, or, as I call it, belly shots with the camera held to the stomach. I am fighting against this viewpoint and shall fight it just as my comrades in the new photography are doing. Take shots from all angles except the navel until all these points of view are recognized. The interesting angles of the present are those from above down and from below up and one must work on those.[46]

Rodchenko acknowledged here the close similarities between his photography and that of Moholy-Nagy or Herbert Bayer. Boris Kusner retorted in *Soviet Photo* that "to show a 150-meter-high radio tower looking

45. Vladimir Lenin, "The Achievements and Difficulties of the Soviet Government" (1919), quoted in Briony Fer, *Russian Art and Revolution* (The Open University: [Modern Art and Modernism], 1983), p. 22.

46. "Novy Lef," 1928, see *Creative Camera*, ed. Colin Osman, 1978.

like a bread basket made of wire is not paying attention to reality but ridiculing facts."

Rodchenko knew that the photograph is no less a sign to be interpreted than any other image—through it reality can be presented and structured in a particular way; this structuring can be made apparent in the use of montage. But this was in direct opposition to the concept of realism advocated by the AKhRR easel painters and the *Soviet Photo* photographers, to which the great majority of posters produced conformed. Klutsis was a major exception. He continued to produce posters well into the Stalinist period, using photography and montage, and also maintaining many of the constructivist design principles. Sometimes, as with the posters built on the symbolic motif of the hand, he took the photograph himself, using documentary photographs which he montaged, or photographs with an angled view. Like Lissitzky's famous Russian exhibition poster (p. 99), heads and whole figures may gaze upwards, but Klutsis usually succeeds in avoiding the potentially idealized, sentimental or utopian nature of this gaze as it tended to be used in the realism of the 30s, by introducing an element of confrontation (train and camel for example), or shock, which depends essentially upon montage.

The appearance of Veshch *(Object) is an indication of the fact that the exchange of 'objects' between young Russian and west European masters has begun. Seven years of separate existence have shown that the community of the tasks and the aims of art in different countries is not something that exists by chance. We are standing in the dawn of a great creative era.*[47]

This opening statement in the first issue of El Lissitzky's and Ilya Ehrenburg's review *Veshch/Gegenstand/Objet* outlines the common aspirations and activities of international Constructivism. The history of its early exhilarating years has often been told, but there are a few specific points I would like to make which bear on my subject. First, there was a significant interaction between dada and Constructivism. Dada was not just an irrational nuisance, to be avoided or stamped out, situated at the opposite pole to Constructivism. There was of course the famous incident when to the horror of the more staid participants it was revealed at the 1922 International Congress of Constructivists in Weimar that Theo van Doesburg and the dada poet I. K. Bonset were one and the same person. But the connections go deeper than that, and the melding of Dadaism and Constructivism created some characteristic and striking "objects:" the special number of Kurt Schwitters's periodical *Merz*, which he designed with El Lissitzky, Schwitters's Merzbau in Hanover, (van Doesburg's) "X-bilden" (X-picture) poems in *De Stijl*, the four issues of Bonset/van Doesburg's *Mécano.* Nor is the dada connection established exclusively through the double participation of Schwitters and van Doesburg in the two movements. Dadaists in Paris like Georges Ribemont-Dessaignes, Francis

Picabia and Paul Eluard contributed to *Mécano*, as did Max Ernst from Cologne, Raoul Hausmann from Berlin. Arp and Tzara contributed to both *Mécano* and to the ex-dadaist Hans Richter's periodical *G*. Richter, now working largely in film, established through the pages of *G* a striking communality of spirit between Constructivism and dada, illustrating, for example, Duchamp's optical disc machine and including poems by Jean Arp and Hausmann as well as articles by Lissitzky, Malevich, Mies van der Rohe and others.

Second, although as *Veshch* had announced general contacts established between Germany and the USSR, and the 1922 exhibition of Soviet art had shown all the major constructivists, El Lissitzky was the dominant influence, particularly on van Doesburg and Moholy-Nagy, and particularly in the field of graphic design. Lissitzky had become a roving cultural ambassador for the new art, but at the same time he was not representative of such groups as the productionists. As he said in *Veshch*: *Obviously we consider that functional objects turned out in factories— aeroplanes and motor cars—are also the product of genuine art. Yet we have no wish to confine artistic creation to these functional objects. Every organized work—whether it be a home, a poem, or a picture—is an 'object' directed toward a particular end, which is calculated not to turn people away from life, but to summon them to make their contribution toward life's organization. . . . Primitive utilitarianism is far from being our doctrine. Objet* (Veshch) *considers poetry, plastic form, theater, as 'objects' that cannot be dispensed with.* [48]

Naum Gabo, who left Russia for good in 1922, totally rejected the "utilitarian" bias of, say, Rodchenko or Klutsis, and it was his view of Constructivism that took root in England and the USA. There were, in other words, a number of different, rather than one monolithic Constructivism.

El Lissitzky's dynamic concept of space, which he explored through the Proun, was eagerly absorbed by Western artists.

I created the Proun as an interchange station between painting and architecture. I have treated the canvas and wooden board as a building site, which placed the fewest restrictions on my constructional ideas. I have used black and white (with flashes of red) as material substance and subject matter. [49]

Building on Malevich's Suprematism (the black square was reproduced on the front of *Veshch* 3), Lissitzky, in the early 1920s, developed his constructive idea based on elementary bodies (cube, cone, sphere), set in "imaginary space:"

47. El Lissitzky and Ilya Ehrenburg, "The Blockade of Russia is Coming to an End," *Veshch/Gegenstand/Objet* nos. 1–2, Berlin, March–April 1922. Trans. in Stephen Bann, *The Tradition of Constructivism* (London: Thames and Hudson, 1974), p. 54.
48. Ibid.
49. Sophie Lissitzky-Küppers, op. cit., p. 325.

Fritz Schleifer
Bauhaus Ausstellung
1923, lithograph
39¾ x 28¾, 101.1 x 73
Collection Merrill C. Berman

Bauhaus Exhibition
Weimar
[dates are listed]
[The symbol of the Bauhaus, a
head of geometric elements,
was designed by Oskar
Schlemmer]

Walter Dexel
Sport
1929, lithograph
33⅛ x 23½, 84.3 x 59.6
Collection Merrill C. Berman

The 1929 sport exhibition in
Magdeburg's exhibition hall on
Lake Adolf-Mittag
Special exhibition by the
German Hygiene Museum
of Dresden
[times and admission fees are
listed]

We saw that the surface of the Proun ceases to be a picture and turns into a structure round which we must circle . . . . The result is that the one axis of the picture which stood at right angles to the horizontal was destroyed. Circling round it, we screw ourselves into space . . . .[50]

Both Moholy-Nagy and van Doesburg were fascinated by El Lissitzky's ideas, and in 1922 he published in *De Stijl*. The result was that the static, flat plane surfaces of De Stijl were spun into space ("We were approaching the state of floating in air and swinging like a pendulum"). In the essentially "closed" fields of pages or posters, Lissitzky's concept of space led to the use of the diagonal, and floating arrangements of words, which were to have a profound influence on graphic design. A special issue of *De Stijl* (October/November 1922) was devoted to drawings and typographical designs by Lissitzky, including the whole "Of 2 Squares," and his article "Topography of Typography" was published by Schwitters in *Merz* 4, July 1923, that emphasized the idea "optics instead of phonetics."

Several factors contributed to the success of international Constructivism. Many of its leading theorists and artists had a pedagogical role. At the Bauhaus, with Gropius and Moholy-Nagy among others, a new generation of designers was trained. For a while, too, van Doesburg had a rogue school at Weimar where he was an important influence in turning the Bauhaus away from the expressionist individualism of Johannes Itten toward the De Stijl version of Constructivism. Second, a number of large international exhibitions were held (of printing at Cologne in 1928, and photography at Stuttgart in 1929, for example) whose catalogues, posters, and so on were designed by a range of constructivist designers. These international exhibitions had a dynamism lost from similar exercises today. Then, there were comparatively good relations with industry, which the Werkbund helped to foster. Finally, there was a steady flow of publications. In 1923, to take the peak year for reviews, there were *Merz, Mécano, Veshch, De Stijl* (published, as it said on the cover, simultaneously in Leiden, Hanover, Paris, Brno, Vienna and Warsaw), *G* and *MA*. From 1925 until 1931 fourteen Bauhaus books were published that were planned and edited by Gropius and Moholy-Nagy. Not only the Bauhaus staff but leading architects and artists all over Europe, including van Doesburg, Moholy-Nagy, Malevich, Schlemmer and Kandinsky contributed theoretical essays.

At the Bauhaus, graphic design grew steadily in importance during the 20s. Initially, while the school was in Weimar, neither typography nor commercial art was actually taught and, though the print workshop was open to students, it was comparatively weak in technical facilities and

50. El Lissitzky, "Proun. Not World Visions BUT— World Reality" *De Stijl,* 1922. Trans. in Sophie Lissitzky-Küppers, op. cit., p. 343.

mainly concerned with the Bauhaus's own printed publicity. When Moholy-Nagy joined the Bauhaus in 1923 he took charge not only of the metal workshop, but also the printing workshop, and encouraged students like Herbert Bayer, Joost Schmidt and Josef Albers to experiment there. Posters were produced for the Bauhaus exhibitions, like Fritz Schleifer's of 1923, with its geometric head constructed from typographical lines and markers, reminiscent of the ex-dadaist Hans Richter's constructivist drawings of heads (p. 58). Oskar Schlemmer, who was in charge of the stage workshop, both at Weimar and Dessau, also worked in the print workshop making posters for his Triadic Ballet. In a 1921 poster for a performance at the Leibniz Academy, Schlemmer used his own costume studies overprinted with different capital typefaces (p. 32). This has an almost anarchic, dada look compared with the rationality of later Bauhaus designs, and Schlemmer remained comparatively untouched by the evolution of graphic design at the Bauhaus. The influence of dada typography is still felt in the invitation for the farewell party of the Weimar Bauhaus in March 1925, before the move to Dessau—a joke for internal consumption, which looks like a sample catalogue of old and new typefaces.

The shift in importance of graphic design by the mid-1920s is reflected in, for example, the course in lettering devised and run by Joost Schmidt, which became a compulsory part of the general education program at Dessau. Success in this area was both technical and commercial. Many firms began to commission Bauhaus designers to produce posters and printed publicity, and also, an important aspect of this field, to design displays and stands for exhibitions.

Bayer, originally a student in the wall-painting workshop, ran the print workshop at Dessau until 1928, when Joost Schmidt took it over, renaming it the Commercial Art Department. Schmidt worked in particular on exhibition design, carrying out displays at large exhibitions such as the Dresden hygiene exhibition of 1928, and a gas and water exhibition for the Junkers Works in 1929. Schmidt favored a restrained, informative and scientific method of presentation. The relationship between displays of this kind, like the poster relying on the mutual supplementation of image and text, and the poster itself, would be interesting to explore further. Schmidt also designed commercial publicity for, for example, cigarette and chocolate manufacturers. Xanti Schawinsky, a student in the mid-20s, who was active on the Bauhaus stage as a designer and an actor, produced posters for clothing and hat manufacturers, and in the 30s for Olivetti (p. 173).

Professional recognition accompanied commercial success, with, for example, the Association of German Advertising Specialists holding part of an instruction course on advertising art in association with the Bauhaus at Dessau in 1927. These factors, together with support from the German Werkbund, contributed to the dominance of modern abstract design on the Continent praised by Barr in 1936.

The stimulus of Moholy-Nagy was crucial. On joining the Bauhaus he immediately directed some of his energy to both the theory and practice of graphic design, in which he emphasized the importance of communication and the immense changes technological advances would bring in this field. His first ideas on typography in the Bauhaus context were published in an article on "The New Typography," in which he stressed clarity and legibility: "Communication must never be impaired by an *a priori* aesthetics. Letters may never be forced into a preconceived framework, for instance, a square."[51] This sounds like an attack on the dogmatic aesthetic of De Stijl, and is a valuable signal to the emphasis placed by the Bauhaus on pragmatic considerations. The rationalization of design and typography was not to be subject to a particular aesthetic program, nor was it to drive out experiment and variation. In the same article of 1923 Moholy wrote: *We use all typefaces, type sizes, geometric forms, colors, etc. We want to create a new language of typography whose elasticity, variability and freshness of typographical composition is exclusively dictated by the inner law of expression and the optical effect.*

Herbert Bayer paid special attention to the creation of a new typography. The Bauhaus had always used the Roman as opposed to the Gothic alphabet, and had often favored sans-serif lettering, but now research was specifically directed toward unified lettering systems, with no distinction between upper and lowercase. A single alphabet would be easier, cheaper and quicker; it would simplify the compositor's job and be more economical in the design of typewriters and typesetting machines. In his 1925 article "Bauhaus and Typography," Moholy-Nagy appealed to precedents, such as the architect Loos, who had written, "One cannot speak a capital letter. Everyone speaks without thinking of capital letters. But when a German takes a pen to write something, he is no longer able to write as he thinks or speaks."[52] The Bauhaus revolution was particularly striking in Germany, where the old, complicated Gothic alphabet was still widely used in printing, with all nouns dignified by the use of capitals, and was greeted with a storm of protest in the press, although, as we noted, commercial firms recognized the enormous advantages for advertising. One of the most significant alphabets was Herbert Bayer's Universal type, based on geometrical shapes, which was widely used on Bauhaus publicity.

The production of radical new typefaces was facilitated at the Bauhaus because every stage of the printing process was under the control of the designers. Particular attention was paid to the demands of large-scale lettering for posters and exhibition displays. Bayer designed a contourless shadow script specifically for use on posters, and Albers designed a stencil

51. L. Moholy-Nagy, "The New Typography" (1923), originally published in *Staatliches Bauhaus in Weimar, 1919–1923.* Trans. in Moholy-Nagy, ed. Richard Kostelanetz (New York: Praeger, 1970), p. 75.
52. Op. cit., p. 76.

abcdefghi
jklmnopqr
stuvwxyz

abcdefghijklmn
opqrſsɈtuvw
xyz

script easily legible from a distance and intended for lettering on billboards. It was constructed from three basic geometric shapes: the square, the triangle as half of the square, and the quarter circle radius. The elements of the letters were placed beside one another without connection, and the unequal sizes of the spaces between the letters were deliberate, "to liven up its appearance as the capital letters in the middle of a word did in the Baroque period."[53] Like Lissitzky, Moholy-Nagy and Bayer tended to use bold lines rather than typographical symbols (which belonged to the "craft-like" mentality of the hand-set type) to aid the clarity and expressive function of the layout in both book and poster design. Bayer sometimes used an additional color, or printed over a tinted base.

Jan Tschichold, an independent typographer who also saw the design of new typefaces as an essential element of graphic design, published the influential book *The New Typography* in 1928. He later criticized Lissitzky for paying insufficient attention to the actual typography of his posters and book designs and, rather, "accepting the conventional shapes of the letters." Much of his work, "original and powerful though it might be, betrays the struggle of the amateur typographer with the ancient, intractable mysteries of printing."[54]

Although attention was paid to typography as an active and fundamental element it would be misleading to suggest that it was at the expense of other elements. Emphasis was on the overall design (with, where relevant, integration of image and text) which Moholy-Nagy characterized as aiming at "dynamic-eccentric equilibrium" as opposed to the "centuries old static-concentric equilibrium." The dynamic overall arrangement (for example, turning the text, or part of it, at 90°) should neither destroy the mutual relationships between the individual elements nor override their legibility.

Attention to the visual impact of typography, which of course at the Bauhaus extended to all printed matter and not just to posters, had in a sense been provoked by the poster. As Moholy-Nagy said:
A new stage of development began with the first posters. . . . One began to count on the fact that form, size, color and arrangement of typographical material (letters and signs) contain a strong visual impact. The organization of these possible visual effects gives a visual validity to the content of the message as well; this means that by means of printing, the content is also being defined pictorially.[55]
The text, in other words, took on the function of the image, and at no other time in the history of the poster, with the exception of dada, had the plasticity of the word been developed so far.

53. Josef Albers. Quoted in Hans M. Wingler, *The Bauhaus* (Cambridge, Mass. and London: The MIT Press, 1969), p. 448.

54. Jan Tschichold, "El Lissitzky (1890–1941)" (1965), Sophie Lissitzky-Küppers, op. cit., p. 355.
55. Ibid.

Frank Newbould
East Coast Frolics No. 6
1933, lithograph
39½ x 25½, 100.3 x 64.7
Collection Victoria and Albert
Museum
acq. no. E.210-1935

Austin Cooper
British Industrial Art
1933, lithograph
30 x 20, 76.2 x 50.8
Collection Victoria and Albert
Museum
acq. no. E.133-1961

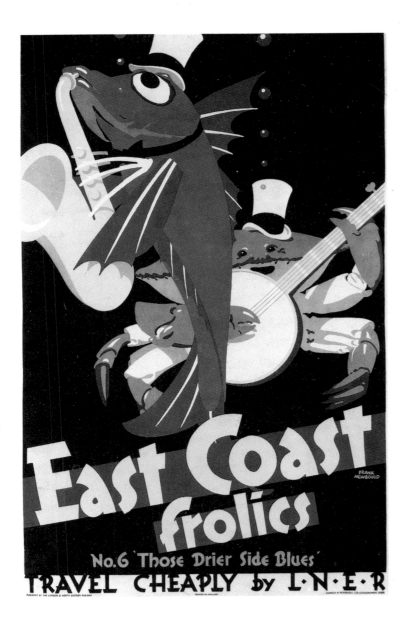

One of the greatest changes in poster production was affected by processes and techniques involving photography. In 1926 Lissitzky looked forward to collotype, the transfer of "composed type matter on to a film, and a printing machine which copies the negative on to sensitive paper." For the first time the same production process would be available for word and illustration. "Letterpress belongs to the past. The future belongs to photogravure printing and to all photomechanical processes. In this way the former fresco painting is cut off from the new typography. E.g.: advertisement pillars and poster walls."[56] Technical journals everywhere, like *Penrose's Annual*, debated the relative merits of the new printing techniques, but the implications in design were only fully realized on the Continent, particularly in Holland and Germany. Moholy-Nagy saw photography as an integral part of poster design:

An equally decisive change in the typographical image will occur in the making of posters, as soon as photography has replaced poster painting. The effective poster must act with immediate impact on all psychological techniques, such as retouching, blocking, superimposition, distorting, enlargement, etc.; in combination with the liberated typographical line, the effectiveness of posters can be immensely enlarged.

The new poster relies on photography, which is the new storytelling device of civilization, combined with the shock effect of new typefaces and brilliant color effects, depending on the desired intensity of the message.[57]

While many constructivist posters still used exclusively typography and abstract geometrical "markers" (Walter Dexel's "Sport" poster of 1929, for example, p. 58), by the end of the decade pictorial elements were increasingly made up of photographs or photomontages. This was particularly appropriate in film posters, and can be seen in the work of, for example, Tschichold and Piet Zwart (pp. 139, 47). Moholy-Nagy's distinctive photomontages, sparser and more structured than the photomontages of Berlin dada, were well suited for poster design and were an important influence on the combining of typography and photographs (see the "Tanz Festspiele" poster, p. 147). The dramatic change is underlined in the 1929 Stuttgart *Film und Foto* exhibition poster (p. 131). Its sharply angled viewpoint derived from the work of Bauhaus photographers like Bayer or Florence Henri, again under the influence of Moholy-Nagy. Bayer included photographs in his posters, which he sometimes printed in non-naturalistic "alienated" colors. During the Bauhaus's brief and threatened life in Berlin from 1932–33, Walter Peterhans was in charge of both the commercial art department (now called the "professional field of advertising") and the photography workshop. This was, by then, a natural alliance, and opportunities increased for designers to work with photography.

Photography and, in particular, photomontage, became a staple both for commercial and political poster designers. For both it could serve as a "fact" in a different way from the representational or expressive character of drawing or painting. The potential of photomontage in building upon or destroying the "factual" nature of reality has been exploited in both commercial and political poster campaigns. The use of the photograph, acceptable to many constructivist designers in a way that figurative painting was not, certainly contributed to the reemergence of a strong pictorial element in posters of the 1930s.

The constructivist attitude to posters was functional in the sense that the medium was expected to fulfill its function efficiently. It demanded clarity, legibility and forcefulness of design, but this was part of a general overhaul of all visual production in accordance with the new technologies. For the constructivists in Russia, in a context where political and social campaigns (to reach production targets, to combat drunkenness) were largely conducted through posters, they had an important ideological function. Within international Constructivism no particular weight was given to the nature of their function.

In England and America, as Barr noted, there was a general failure to adopt modernist design, but, parallel to the vision of a new society pushed by the constructivists with a crusading zeal, there was a feeling that a new age was dawning in which the poster had an important role. Nowhere is this clearer than in Calvin Coolidge's address in 1926 to the American Association of Advertising Agencies. He accorded commercial advertising a potentially utopian function: it "makes new thoughts, new desires, new actions," and "by changing the attitude of mind it changes the material condition of people," but it is idealistic according to the ideals of capitalism, for the educational or informational role of advertising is dependent upon its commercial function: "advertising ministers to the spiritual side of trade."[58]

As E. McKnight Kauffer wrote in *The Art of the Poster*, the commercial dominates completely. His statement in the first issue of the *Bulletin* of the newly formed Arts League of Service, in 1919, is obviously trying to shift the function of the poster away from pure commercialism, but is vague about what might go in its place:

Few people realize the importance of the hoardings. It is from them that the masses gather ideas for a great many things that directly influence them. Now that England, after a pause of a dozen years, is again interested in the poster, let this feeling be so genuine and broadcast as to make the hoardings amusingly interesting and vitally important.[59]

56. El Lissitzky, "Typographical Facts" (1925), Sophie Lissitzky-Küppers, op. cit., p. 355.
57. L. Moholy-Nagy, "The New Typography," op. cit.
58. Calvin Coolidge address delivered at the annual convention of the American Association of Advertising Agencies at Washington, D. C., 27 October 1926. Quoted in Frank Presbrey, *The History and Development of Advertising* (New York: Doubleday, Devan & Co., 1929).

Only a handful of people were concerned to make the hoardings "amusingly interesting." Of these, in England, the most dynamic and influential was Frank Pick, who was in charge of publicity for the Underground Railway Company from 1908. Not only did he carefully organize the advertising space inside and at the entrances to his stations, but he began a policy of commissioning designers to produce posters on specific themes: rural England within reach of the city dweller, museums and galleries, winter sales, all available through this means of cheap and efficient transport. He selected the best designers, and even commissioned a new alphabet in 1913 from the calligrapher Edward Johnston, and, when it appeared in 1916, the Johnston sans serif was revolutionary.

Kauffer, the best of his designers, had no illusions about the philanthropic nature of his intentions, however, and in 1926 Roger Fry had some acid comments to make about such campaigns:

The big companies pose as the friends and advisers of the public, they appear filled with concern about their welfare, they would even educate them, and show them the way to higher and better things. The Underground tells the slum dweller of the beauties of nature in the country, it reveals the wonders of animal life at the zoo, it inspires the historical sense by pictures of old London . . .

No doubt this has got to do with another interesting recent discovery of commerce. The early industrialist believed in increasing output and decreasing price. For some reason the modern industrialist finds his advantage in restricting output and increasing price. Advertisement is used not so much to induce us to buy as to make us willing to pay more for things than they cost to produce. Thus the railway companies give us progressively worse and worse accommodation but, by advertisement, they produce in the public a non-critical state of romantic enthusiasm for the line . . .[60]

Having thus attacked the invidious and illusionary nature of "the spiritual side of advertising," Fry goes on to suggest that a possible way out for the advertisers is to turn their "philanthropy" not to the public but to artists. Having driven them out of the field of designing textiles, pottery, etc. through mass production, business could re-create a role for the designer of posters, because the poster is a relatively inexpensive object to produce, and the industrialist would not be taking the same risks as he would in setting up the design of objects for large-scale and expensive production. The poster could, he suggests, become a medium in its own right within the field of "opifacts:"

59. Quoted in Mark Haworth-Booth, *E. McKnight Kauffer: A Designer and His Public* (London: Gordon Fraser, 1979), p. 29.

60. Roger Fry, *Art and Commerce* (London: Hogarth Press, 1926), originally given as a lecture on the occasion of an ALS poster exhibition at Oxford, 1925.

A. M. Cassandre
Wagon-Bar
1932, offset lithograph with
lithograph
39½ x 24½, 100.3 x 62.4
Collection Merrill C. Berman

Restore yourself in the wagon-
bar.

Soaring to Success !

DAILY HERALD

— the Early Bird.

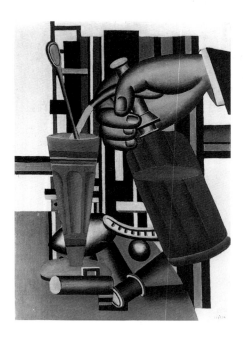

There is as yet no Royal Academy of Poster Designers, there is no fixed and traditional notion of the kind of thing a poster ought to be. There is as yet no pedantry, no culture, no lecturing, until tonight to hamper and harass the man who happens to have a gift in this medium.

Fry was in fact not quite right, for there had been a Poster Academy, founded in 1901, when poster magazines and societies had flourished, but when these faded away the poster had remained in an undeveloped state. Fry was apparently unaware of the new theories of graphic design associated with Constructivism, but was conscious of a revitalization in this "new opifact industry" involving "experiments in the possibilities of printing, and in the effect of color arrangements."

McKnight Kauffer had the reputation in England of having helped to convert the public to modern art. He was often indeed taken by conservative opponents like the advertising manager of Pears Soap as an example of extreme and incomprehensible modernism. But Kauffer himself was quite aware of the mildness of his "modernism:"

The terms 'cubistic,' 'futuristic' and the like are too often applied to the present day poster in error. Practically in every case these terms are confused by the user, and to many advertising people the use of them produces a shudder of fear. They somehow suggest that such ideas and the users are slightly, if not entirely insane. The antipathy to newer developments in design and color has its reason, no doubt, but I am bound to say, with but two or three exceptions, no such design has made its appearance, in England at any rate. For my part, the brief research I have made in these movements as a painter, has been very beneficial to me in the designing of posters. It has made it possible to make newer translations of old forms, and it has assisted me to emphasize the qualities and importance of the use of color, and helped to simplify my arrangements of ideas.[61]

Kauffer was closely associated with Wyndham Lewis (whose use of bold uppercase typography in *Blast* was praised as a forerunner by Lissitzky) in his early career as a painter. One of his best designs, a poster for the *Daily Herald*, based on a woodcut called *Flight*, is close to Vorticism in its flat but dynamic abstraction of birds. After he devoted himself to poster design, the links between his work and modern painting become, as he suggested, pragmatic. It is possible to pick out certain specific influences in certain posters, such as Delaunay's color discs, but on the whole the influence is very general, prompting him towards flattening form and simplifying color. The book jacket for H. G. Wells's *The Open Conspiracy,* 1929, with the diagonal slant to the typography, and the use of abstract typographical

61. E. McKnight Kauffer, "The Poster and Symbolism," *Penrose's Annual,* 1924.

E. McKnight Kauffer
Daily Herald
1918, lithograph
(n.i.e.)
Collection Victoria and Albert
Museum

Fernand Léger
Le Syphon
1924, oil on canvas
(n.i.e.)
Collection Albright-Knox Art
Gallery
Gift of Mr. and Mrs. Gordon
Bunshaft

Dawn Ades is presently lecturer

in the history of art at Essex

University, Colchester. Her

books include *Photomontage*,

1976, *Dada and Surrealism*

Reviewed*, 1978, and *Salvador

***Dali*, 1982.**

markers like the circle and rectangle, show that he was familiar with some constructivist design, and he used diagonally set typography several times—for Imperial Airways, or the post office telephone series, in other words where he felt it would be effective and significant, but by no means as an invariable aesthetic principle.

He believed that the symbol was the essential element in poster design, which would be simple and swiftly recognized. In this he was not unlike Cassandre, and both owe a certain debt to the purists Ozenfant and Jeanneret, in their adoption of a vocabulary of simple forms. Both Kauffer and Cassandre recognized that there was an essential difference between the function of a poster and the function of a painting, and that the conception must therefore be different too. The dangers of ignoring this simple fact are evident in some of the Shell posters of the 1930s. In 1933 Shell approached a number of artists in their studios to produce posters on the theme "Everywhere you go you can be sure of Shell." *Commercial Art and Industry* published the results under the title "A Great Adventure in Posters." Those that do not work are those that are simply a transposition—not even a translation—of a picture into a poster.

Poster design in Paris had on the whole remained decorative, often using flat colorful patterned abstractions with exotic overtones. A.M. Cassandre, like Kauffer in England, was the most imaginative and successful in adapting contemporary development in painting to posters. Unlike Herbin, who favored a flat decorative abstract style, Cassandre always based his design on people or objects, however dramatically reduced or simplified they might be. Cassandre's affinities lie above all with Léger and the purists. The "Wagon-Bar" poster of 1932 plays on the purist concept of basing a pictorial language on the forms of certain manufactured objects, which, because they are geometrical, are perceived as closer to pure or ideal form. This poster could be compared with Léger's painting of a soda siphon. Like that, it is a slightly tongue-in-cheek homage to Purism, and demonstrates again how various abstract and constructivist ideas, in theory and practice, acted upon poster design, and how, reciprocally, the special, practical demands of the poster tested and provided the impetus for these ideas.

The important thing is to find a silhouette that is expressive, a symbol which, simply by its form and colors, can force its attention on a crowd and dominate the passer-by.

Maurice Denis

The development of the Russian film poster marked a high point in Russian avant-garde art in the 1920s. From 1925 to 1929, in particular, it reached a level of innovation and expressiveness that has yet to be surpassed in the Soviet Union or in the West.[1]

Film posters first appeared in Russia in the late 1890s and spread along with the growing film industry.[2] Following the lead of the dramatic theaters, the earliest posters were simply printed announcements. However it wasn't long before enterprising promoters sought ways to distinguish their advertisements from those of their competitors through the addition of illustrations. The quality of the early film posters depended largely on the taste and resources of the film promoter and the artist he happened to choose. There were no professional film-poster designers. In general, the poster was regarded as outside the realm of serious art, which, until 1918 was firmly in the hands of conservative academicians.[3]

Those illustrated film posters that were produced in Russia during the first two decades of this century tended toward a folkloristic style reflecting

1. Grateful acknowledgment is made to the authors of the collection of articles in *Sovetskii kinoplakat,* ed. V.A. Tikhanova, (Moscow: Sovetskii khudozhnik, 1961), for the wealth of information they have provided on the early development of the Russian film poster. I also wish to express my indebtedness to Mildred Constantine and Alan Fern's pioneering work, *Revolutionary Soviet Film Posters,* (Baltimore and London: The Johns Hopkins University Press, 1974).
2. Lumière's Cinématographe was presented at the "Aquarium," a summer theater in St. Petersburg in May 1896. The first Russian movie house was opened two days later in the same city. For additional information on the history of the film industry in Russia see Jay Leyda, *Kino. A History of Russian and Soviet Film,* (London: Allen and Unwin, 1960).
3. This attitude prevails today in the Soviet Union and has led to the paradoxical situation that permits more freedom to designers of all kinds than to painters or sculptors to experiment with avant-garde forms.

(p. 70)
Stenberg brothers
The Eleventh
1928, lithograph
39⅞ x 26¾, 101.2 x 68
Collection Merrill C. Berman

Author and Director:
Dziga Vertov
Cameraman: Mikhail Kaufman

[The title is a reference to the
11th anniversary of the
Revolution.]

the influence of the traditional lubok or peasant broadside. They revealed little direct awareness of the development abroad of the poster form. The arresting works of the great French artists, Jules Chéret, Pierre Bonnard, Toulouse-Lautrec, and those of innumerable artists of the Art Nouveau movement were not widely known in Russia. Nor, for that matter, did they reflect the influence on Russian graphic art, particularly book cover design, of those artists affiliated with the World of Art movement, many of whom also designed posters.

A striking exception to the low level of early film posters was a group created by the artist and poet, Vladimir Mayakovsky, for the private firm, Neptune, where he worked briefly as both scriptwriter and actor.[4] The poet's posters for the films *Not Born for Money* and *Shackled by Film*, both produced in 1918, stood out because of their sophisticated use of graphic techniques and imagery, reflecting the artist's awareness of Western poster art and the influence on his work of the Art Nouveau. This is especially true of the poster for *Shackled by Film* in which a sinuous green curve of film curls up from a reel to entwine the hands of the heroine whose head rises like some exotic flower from a red heart.

World War I and the Revolution brought a significant change to the film poster as it did to all Russian art. Art moved out into the streets to become a powerful propaganda medium in the service of the new society. The constructivist movement introduced a new aesthetic that replaced decoration with functionalism and called for a simple, colorful, easily-remembered imagery. Film itself was declared "the most important art," and everything possible was done to encourage its development.[5]

However, in spite of the rapid growth of the film industry after the Revolution and the large number of foreign films imported during the NEP (New Economic Policy) period to satisfy the appetite of a growing public, the film poster continued to be a haphazard affair at best. Posters whose stylized form and mastery of graphics reflected the changing aesthetics of the post-Revolutionary period were still few and far between. As in the West, artists concentrated on advertising the film's stars or depicting one of the episodes in the picture. Posters such as the one by an unknown artist for Erich von Stroheim's *Foolish Wives*, 1925, differ little from their Western counterparts in the banality of their composition. Few of these early artists were as successful as those of the 1920s would be in incorporating the recognizable image of a popular star into their posters in a way that was graphically effective.

In appealing to a largely bourgeois audience, these early poster artists

4. Mayakovsky recognized the importance of film as early as 1913 when he stated, "Theater will bring its own demise and must pass on its heritage to the cinema." Mayakovsky, *Sobranie sochenenii v dvenadsati tomakh* XI (Moscow: Izd. Pravda, 1978), p. 7.
5. Leyda, p. 170

frequently relied on dramatic incidents and melodramatic effects. Many of them simply borrowed the form and graphics of the political posters of the period, making liberal use of allegory and symbolism. Posters abounded with images of the devil, death and dragons. A typical example can be seen in the 1924 poster by an unknown artist for *Red Partisans,* which depicts the red silhouette of a figure energetically waving his sword at a huge green dragon. But whereas in political posters such allegorical figures seemed quite appropriate, they were usually out of place in film posters which frequently bore little if any relationship to the content of a film.

Often, especially in the case of imported films, the artists had to rely on publicity photographs and a brief synopsis, so they often failed to understand what a film was about. At times, however, it was a matter of salesmanship overcoming truth, a practice that continued well into the 1920s. For example, in an effort to create a more sensational poster for Pudovkin's 1926 film *Mother,* the artist Iosif Bograd took a frame showing Nilova embracing her son Pavel's legs as she tries to stop him from taking weapons hidden under the floor. Bograd transformed this powerfully emotional scene into a political indictment by showing the heroine pressing her face to a policeman's boot as she tries to stop him from arresting her son.

The year 1924 was a turning point in the development of the Russian film poster. With the abolition of all private film companies the previous year, the first steps were taken to centralize all film production and distribution in the Russian Republic under a single organization, Goskino (after 1926, Sovkino).[6] And in an effort to systematize the production of film posters, a separate department, Reklam Film, was organized, headed by Yakov Rukhlevsky. Rukhlevsky soon put together a group of young poster artists, many of whom were former students at Vkhutemas (Higher State Art-Technical Studios). They included, in addition to Rukhlevsky, the brothers Vladimir and Georgii Stenberg, Nikolai Prusakov, Aleksandr Naumov, Mikhail Dlugach, Leonid Voronov, Grigory Rychkov, Grigory Borisov, Iosif Bograd and Iosif Gerasimovich.[7]

6. Sovkino was the most powerful of the national film organizations in the mid-1920s. In addition to controlling the distribution of all foreign films, Sovkino had three film studios (or factories as they were then called) in Moscow employing ten groups of film producers and one in Leningrad employing twelve groups. Many of these groups had their own film poster departments. Other national monopolies, each of which also had its own film poster department, included "Goskinprom" Gruzii (the Georgian film organization), VUFKU (All-Ukranian Photo-Cinema Administration), "Bukhkino" (in Uzbekistan) and "Belgoskino" (in Byelorussia).

(Leyda p. 167; see also "Kino," *Entsiklopedicheskii spravochnik SSSR,* ed. A.M. Prokhorov et al (Moscow: Sovetskaia entsiklopoediia, 1982), p. 505; and *Film und Filmkunst in der USSR 1917–1928* [published by VOKS (the USSR Society for Cultural Relations with Foreign Countries), n.d.]).

7. "The Soviet Film Poster's First Steps" (Pervye shagi sovetskogo kinoplakat), *Sovetskii kinoplakat,* p. 6. Of the original members of the group, only Gerasimovich and Dlugach are still living. The latter continues to work, mainly designing propaganda posters. He made his last film poster in 1980.

Stenberg brothers
Man with a Movie Camera
1929, lithograph
41⅛ x 26⅛, 104.5 x 66.4
Collection Elaine Lustig Cohen

Author and Director:
Dziga Vertov
Chief cinematographer:
Mikhail Kaufman
Assistant Editor for Montage:
Yelizaveta Svilova

A film without words
[in innermost circle]

Stenberg brothers
The Three-Million Dollar Case
1926, lithograph
38⅞ x 27½, 98.7 x 70
Collection Merrill C. Berman

A comedy
Director: Yakob A. Protozanov

Stenberg brothers
A Screw from Another Machine
1927, lithograph
42⅜ x 28⅝, 107.5 x 72.8
Collection Merrill C. Berman

A tragicomedy in twenty days
Director: Talanov
Cameraman: Minervin
Starring: A. N. Paramonova and
P. P. Repnin
[the above words are on the hat
band]

The new film posters were characterized by an extraordinary dynamism. They were far more colorful than their pre-Revolutionary and early post-Revolutionary antecedents and they attracted the spectator with their inventiveness and originality. Instead of timidly copying a film frame, these artists attempted to draw from a more considered selection of plot situations. And gradually, as they better understood the nature of the film genre, they turned more and more away from a depiction of the obvious, narrative features of a film, to seek ways to reveal its more subtle, psychological meaning.

The techniques of film itself became the raw material for film posters. Many of the artists made use of the close-up, the face of the film's hero often occupying almost the entire area of the poster. Montage, which in the 1920s was one of the most influential elements of cinema technique adopted by many theatrical and graphic artists, also became one of the basic graphic devices in the film poster. It frequently took the form of a split poster showing a juxtaposition of images as in the Stenberg brothers' poster for *A Screw from Another Machine,* 1927 which combines a close-up of the hero with a long shot of two checker-suited city slickers. Another favorite device for conveying the sense of a moving picture was the use of repetition, frequently an important design element, as in the case of the locomotives in the Stenbergs' poster for the Buster Keaton film *The General*, 1928.

Among the group of designers who worked for Sovkino, Georgii and Vladimir Stenberg were without parallel. The brothers, who had already made a name for themselves as leading members of the constructivist movement and as scenic designers at the Moscow Kamerny Theatre, began designing film posters in 1924. The highly original poster Vladimir Stenberg had created the previous year for the Kamerny Theatre's tour in Paris (p. 121) had already excited considerable attention by the time the brothers were asked to create a poster for the foreign film, *The Eyes of Love*. The Stenbergs' work immediately stood out because of its economical means of expression and extraordinary feeling for color. Before long, the brothers had become two of the major figures in the film-poster world, and posters bearing the signature, 2 Stenberg 2, could be seen everywhere.[8]

The Stenbergs placed great emphasis on constructivist principles in their poster work. They were masters at transforming the surface of the poster into a dynamic composition which seems to project from the poster to grab the viewer's attention as, for example, in their poster for *Turksib,*

8. The brothers signed this first poster "Sten," because, as Vladimir Stenberg explained, they weren't certain whether they would do any more film posters. For additional information on the Stenbergs' artistic activities see Alma H. Law, "A Conversation with Vladimir Stenberg," *Art Journal*, Fall 1981, pp. 222–233; and Selim O. Khan-Magomedov, "Brat'ia Stenbergi" (The Stenberg Brothers), *Tekhnicheskaia estetika*, No. 10, 1982, pp. 22–27.

which is dominated by an onrushing locomotive. Obversely, in *Man with a Movie Camera (Chelovek c kino apparatum)*, 1929 (p. 74), the composition seems to swirl inward, drawing the viewer into the depths of the image.

The Stenbergs rarely used photomontage, preferring instead tosimulate by artistic means an almost photolike image. Unlike their predecessors, who would take a still photograph and mark it into squares in order to transfer the portrait to their poster maquette—in much the same way billboard painters work—the brothers devised more efficient mechanical means for projecting the image directly onto the paper, thus enabling them to capture quickly and accurately a portrait likeness for their poster. The result, particularly in those works dominated by a head shot, as for example, the one for the 1926 comedy, *The Three-Million Dollar Case* (p. 75), was more lifelike than an actual photograph would have been. As Vladimir Stenberg later recalled, "We would give the most attention to the eyes and the nose . . . . There would be nothing superfluous . . . ."[9]

A brilliant exception can be seen in their use of photomontage in the poster for Dziga Vertov's 1928 documentary film, *The Eleventh (Odinnadtsati)* (p. 70), in which the lens of the eyeglasses reflect photographic images of factory machinery. In all of their posters, however, the Stenbergs make great use of the devices of cinematic montage such as repetition or the use of two sharply contrasting images juxtaposed for dramatic effect, as in their poster for *Chicago,* 1928 (p. 78), where the laughing heroine in the upper right is counterbalanced in mood by the threatening image at lower left of a gangster holding a smoking pistol. The brothers' posters also frequently reflect the cinema's fascination with unusual camera angles, as in their 1926 design for *Katka's Reinette Apples,* suggesting an aerial shot of a stairwell.

The Stenbergs were also pioneers in the use of unusual color combinations, a quality frequently noted by Western critics of the period. They had a keen understanding of the lithographic process and were able to take full advantage of its potential in creating a broad palate with the minimum means at their disposal. They also pioneered in breaking away from the traditional white background, daring even to place their design against black as, for example, in their dramatic treatment of the heroine in their poster for *Moulin Rouge*, 1929. They had an unfailing sense of ways to make their posters stand out from the myriad of others pasted on walls and fences. While an image might occupy the entire area of one of their posters, they were equally capable of doing just the opposite—of placing a very small composition in the center of an otherwise bare poster.

Composition was one of the Stenberg brothers greatest strengths. And

9. In conversation with the writer, 7 June 1981.

Stenberg brothers
Chicago
1928, lithograph
35⅝ x 23⅛, 90.7 x 58.7
Collection Merrill C. Berman

Stenberg brothers
High Society Wager
1927, lithograph
40 x 27, 101.7 x 68.5
Collection Merrill C. Berman

A film drama by Sovkino

at the viewer as if seen through a keyhole.[11] Rodchenko's other film posters include his 1925 designs for *Battleship Potemkin* and his 1926 poster for Vertov's *One Sixth of the World.*

Nikolai Prusakov, a member of the same artistic circle as Rodchenko and the Stenberg brothers, was responsible for some of the most inventive posters of the period, combining caricature and dadalike effects, photomontage and multiple imagery. His fascination with kinetic forms, going back as early as 1921 when he constructed a moving bas-relief, found frequent expression in his poster designs. For *Khaz-Push*, 1927 (p. 82), designed in collaboration with Grigory Borisov, Prusakov makes brilliant use of photomontage to create a man on a bicycle hurrying to see the film. This is also one of the rare examples of a Russian film poster with a text that reads like advertising copy: "I am hurrying to see *Khaz-Push*."

Prusakov frequently drew on unexpected juxtapositions, as in his poster for the film *Bureaucrats and People*, 1929, based on a work by Anton Chekhov. It shows a woman wearing an upturned carriage on her head. Below is a multiple-faced bureaucrat supported by a pair of spectacles. This same sense of absurdity informs his poster for the satirical film, *The Woman Outsider*, 1929, where a face becomes a dancing figure. Prusakov's use of the automobile in his posters, most notably in *The House on Trubna Street*, 1928 (in collaboration with Grigory Borisov), *Five Minutes that Shook the World*, 1929, and *Great Tragedy for a Small Woman*, 1929, reveal his fondness for this archetypal image of urban life. Unfortunately, by the 1930s, Prusakov's work fell under increasing suspicion for its "formalist" tendencies so that few examples of it remain today.

Although his career was cut short in 1928, when he perished in a drowning accident, Aleksandr Naumov also showed great promise as an imaginative and innovative poster designer as evidenced in such works as *Bella Donna*, 1927, and *Her Husband's Trademark*, 1925. Like Prusakov and Borisov, Naumov experimented with optical vibration, the breaking down of the surface by means of hand-drawn screens in order to create a sense of three-dimensionality.

One of the most prolific of the film poster artists was Mikhail Dlugach. A native of Kiev, where he had studied architecture, Dlugach began designing film posters full-time in 1925. In the course of his long career as a graphic artist he produced posters for more than five hundred films. Perhaps the most noteworthy of his works during the 1920s are his distinctive black and yellow design for Ernst Lubitsch's *The Oyster Princess* in 1926, and his poster for *Cement*, 1928, combining constructivist motifs and montage effects.

Of the other poster artists active in the second half of the 1920s, few were able to produce with any consistency posters that were of lasting artistic value. Unlike the Stenbergs, many of these artists were initially handicapped by a lack of knowledge of basic lithography techniques so that

Nikolai Prusakov and Grigory
Borisov
Khaz-Push
1927, lithograph
27⅝ x 41¾, 70.3 x 106.2
Collection Merrill C. Berman

I am Hurrying to see *Khaz-Push*
[A Soviet-Armenian film about
the struggle in the 1890s
between Russia and England for
the Persian market. The Khaz-
Push were the proletarianized
Persian peasants and craftsmen
who fought against foreign
control of Persia.]

Stenberg brothers
Fragment of an Empire
1929, lithograph
37⅛ x 24½, 94.2 x 62.3
Collection Merrill C. Berman

Sovkino, Leningrad
Director: Friedrich Ermler

[other credits are listed on the
right-hand edge]

they were unable to take full advantage of the possibilities of this medium. With some notable exceptions, many of their designs simply imitated, but with far less success, the techniques and devices pioneered by the Stenberg brothers.

Some artists, like Mikhail Evstafyev, Iosif Bograd and Leonid Voronov, who was nicknamed "the fireman" by his fellow artists because of the speed with which he could execute a design, tended to work in a realistic vein, producing posters that were frequently overburdened with narrative detail. An exception was the 1927 design created by Evstafyev and Voronov for *October* in which they very successfully combine several diverse images from the film, dramatically uniting them with a zigzag line that cuts diagonally across the poster like a bolt of lightning.

Anatoly Belsky preferred, on the other hand, to concentrate on an image of a single character in a film. For *The Communar's Pipe,* 1929, he chose a headshot of the young hero, who is killed because he refuses to part with his father's pipe, depicting the subject of the film, the Paris Commune, in the form of smoke emanating from the pipe. Though striking in itself, this mannerism often seems curiously out of tune with the theme of the film being advertised. For example, in spite of its being a fine example of urban imagery—the head of a man in top hat angled against a skyscraper—one cannot help but puzzle over this choice for his poster *Five Minutes*, 1929 (p. 128), a film whose title is a reference to the five-minute work stoppage observed at the time of Lenin's interment.

The problems facing these early film-poster designers were monumental. Not only did they have to meet the demands of a distributor who was trying to squeeze out a maximum profit for each film, but they had to carry them out under the most difficult conditions. Frequently the artists had to work against unbelievable deadlines. Both Vladimir Stenberg and Mikhail Dlugach recall that it was not at all unusual to see a film at three in the afternoon and be obliged to produce a finished poster by ten the following morning.[12]

The artists were also limited in the technical means at their disposal. The only presses available were pre-Revolutionary ones that printed from a flat stone, and as Vladimir Stenberg noted, "Some of these machines were so shaky that practically everything was held together by strings."[13] In addition, there were periods when paper was in short supply, and the posters, usually printed in a *tirage* of ten to twenty-thousand copies, would have to be made on half sheets.[14] Dlugach also recalls a time when the only paper available was the dull gray kind used for book covers.[15] None of these

12. Stenberg, in conversation, 7 June 1981; Dlugach, in conversation, 17 June 1981.
13. In conversation, 7 June 1981.

14. The usual size of a poster made from a single sheet of poster paper was approximately 100 x 75 cm (40 x 28 in).
15. In conversation, 6 February 1982.

problems, however, seemed to stem the avalanche of film posters, and with each new film, billboards and building walls were adorned with these posters, at times threatening to drive out all other forms of advertising.

Two basic tendencies are seen in the posters of the 1920s: first, the attempt to convey a film's plot, the dramatic conflict or the relationship between the characters, by means of a juxtaposition of images depicting highlights of the film; the second tendency was the selection of a single moment or characteristic image to dominate the poster. An eminently successful example of the latter was the poster by the Stenbergs for Dovzhenko's film-poem *Arsenal*, 1929, which depicts, against a dark purple background, the figure of a soldier staggering backwards as he tries to ward off a gas attack. Sometimes, the artist would select an image that already carried with it a highly charged meaning, as did Iosif Bograd in his poster advertising Pudovkin's *The End of St. Petersburg*, 1928, on which he placed against a red background the famous equestrian statue of Alexander III, known to everyone as the "Scarecrow."

Some of the best posters in the second half of the 1920s were inspired by the films of such leading directors as Eisenstein, Dovzhenko, particularly those films based on revolutionary themes. The posters designed by the Stenberg brothers, Anton Lavinsky, and Rodchenko for Eisenstein's *Battleship Potemkin 1905,* although widely different in style, marked a high point in Russian poster art. It is instructive to compare the Stenbergs' extremely laconic design of crossed cannons against a red and blue background, so closely paralleling Eisenstein's fascination with diagonal film composition, with Rodchenko's radically different interpretation in his two posters. In the first of his posters, Rodchenko also concentrates on pure design, framing the two guns of the battleship in a diamond-shaped pattern, which in seeming to extend beyond the edge of the paper creates a peculiarly disorienting sensation in the viewer. For his other poster Rodchenko evokes a curious inside-outside effect by placing two scenes from the film (the sailor falling overboard, and sailors turning the gun turret toward the viewer) within two portholes. Of an entirely different order is Anton Lavinsky's poster that uses an actual shot from the film: the head of a sailor, with the muzzles of the ship's guns aimed right at the viewer. The energy of the sailor's shout of "Man overboard!" is reinforced by the pattern of wires and ropes in the background, making this one of the most successful posters of the period (p. 87).

Equally outstanding was the 1927 poster the Stenberg brothers and Yakov Rukhlevsky designed for Eisenstein's film, *October.* Metaphorically descriptive of the events of the October Revolution, the poster shows the Czar's emblematic eagle being toppled. At the left side, the Battleship Aurora is shown, and across the bottom, Rukhlevsky contributed a frieze that depicts men pulling a cannon. One can only guess at the stunning effect this monumental poster must have had (it measured 264 by 204 cm.

Stenberg brothers
Battleship Potemkin 1905
1929, lithograph
[for Sovkino reissue of 1925 film
by Goskino]
35⅜ x 26⅜, 90 x 67
Collection Merrill C. Berman

Director: Sergei Eisenstein
Cameraman: Eduard Tisse

Anton Lavinsky
Battleship Potemkin 1905
1925, lithograph
27⅝ x 41⅞, 70.2 x 106.5
Collection Merrill C. Berman

The pride of Soviet cinema
Goskino, 1925
Director: Sergei Eisenstein
Cameraman: Eduard Tisse

[19 x 15 feet]), especially when shown in series, as was often the practice on the sides of buildings.

Many film posters reflected the constructivist fascination with the machine and modern technology. In the late 1920s, airplanes, automobiles, skyscrapers, smokestacks and other forms of urban imagery dominated the work of the leading poster designers. The Stenberg brothers were pioneers in the use of the latter and their posters featuring skyscrapers and other icons of urban life were widely imitated.

Letterforms and typography also served as raw material for the designers of the Russian posters, reflecting a fascination that harks back to pre-Revolutionary work of the cubo-futurists. Especially worthy of note is the 1931 anonymous constructivist image for Vertov's first sound film, *Enthusiasm*, which repeats in vibrantly colorful lettering the film's title in concentric circles emanating from a camera lens. Both Borisov and Zhukov's poster for *The Living Corpse*, 1929, and Gerasimovich's *Prince Charming*, 1929, use letters of the alphabet as a basic design element. This fascination with letterforms can also be seen in the Stenberg brothers' posters for *Moulin Rouge*, 1929, and *The Shooting of Dan McGrew*, 1927, where they combine a variety of Cyrillic and Roman type forms. The Stenbergs also pioneered in creating their own dramatically simple constructivist type style which became known among the poster designers as "Stenberg lettering."

The most accomplished designers placed an emphasis on conveying the particularity of a film's genre. They strove to have not only the images but also the artistic language of a poster dictated by the film. Least successful, in general, were the posters for films on contemporary subjects, especially comedies. In part this was because of the poor quality of many of these films which offered little nourishment to feed the artist's imagination. There were exceptions, however, and some of the posters for film comedies are distinguished by a finely tuned wittiness. The Stenbergs, for example, didn't hesitate to turn a figure upside down, as in the Pat and Patashon poster for *Public Idol*, or to turn two figures into the arms of a windmill, as in the poster for *The Riddle of the Windmill.* Similarly, Dlugach's poster for *Trio* very successfully conveys the satirical character of this comedy, not only through the accentuation of characteristic details, but also through the use of sharply defined cartoonlike images.

Although little information is available about the work of Leningrad film-poster artists during the 1920s, those few examples that have come to light are characterized by a high degree of artistic inventiveness. The topsy-turvy montage of images in the 1924 poster for *The Adventures of Oktyabrina*, a fantasy film created by FEKS (The Factory of the Eccentric

16. Leyda, *Kino*, p. 180.
17. "Soveshchanie khudoznikov plakatistov o sovetskoi kinoreklame," *Pechat i revoliutsiia*, Book 5–6 (May–June 1930).

Actor) directors Grigori Kozintsev and Leonid Trauberg, clearly reflects the film's upside-down world in which, as Jay Leyda recalls, "The least pretentious episode I remember from it is a crowd bicycling across roofs!"[16] Another noteworthy poster to come out of Leningrad during the 1920s is Wechsler's striking example of suprematist poster art for Eduard Johanson and Friedrich Ermler's 1926 film *Children of the Storm* (p. 134).

By the end of the 1920s the output of Soviet films had grown significantly, and the government began restricting the number of foreign imports. Increased governmental control of the arts in the post-NEP period also had its effect on the film poster. In large part this grew out of an increased awareness of the power of the poster both as a propaganda and as an educational tool. As a directive in 1931 stated, "Because the Soviet film poster, as an indivisible part of the political-educational work of the cinema, has as its basic objective the popularization and promotion of the Soviet film output for the masses, [we] recognize the necessity for [film] advertising to express clearly the political objective of the film, and in its design actively to affect the mass spectator and decisively to dissassociate itself from the old methods of advertising which led to the pandering of bourgeois taste."[17]

The question of the social role of the film poster had been raised as early as 1925, in a debate following the first exhibition of film posters that year. With the advent of Socialist Realism in the early 1930s, under which subject matter and artistic means were required to be "true to life," came the ascendance of realism over the dramatic experimentation of the 1920s. It marked the end of the great innovative period of the Soviet film poster and of one of the most exciting movements in the history of graphic design.

Alma Law is a theater historian with a special interest in 20th-century Russian culture. She is affiliated with the Center for Advanced Study in Theater Arts, City University Graduate Center, New York.

Basler Freilichtspiele
beim Letziturm im St. Albantal
15.-31. VIII 1963

Wilhelm Tell

In the history of visual communication, we see that almost all important technical discoveries of the past have found their way into industries dealing with visual reproduction. In fact, technical innovations affect society in no other domain so quickly and so radically as here, where human beings convey to others their knowledge, insights, inventions and plans.

Before movable type was a possibility for communication, one was restricted to the reproduction of simple information through wood engraving. We are all aware of the enormous social changes experienced during the Middle Ages due to the subsequent technology provided by letterpress printing. In the centuries that followed, the surface characteristics of the printing carrier improved. Etching and copperplate engraving allowed for more sophisticated statements, but the speed and quantity of that printing was not substantially greater than it had been with wood engraving and the block letter. Only lithography, which developed in the middle of the 19th century, enabled reproduction techniques to cope with the tasks that were imposed by the onset of the industrial age through:

1. the ability to make more complex statements
2. the introduction of a wider range of colors
3. faster production
4. the use of larger formats
5. wider circulation

Any discussion concerning the future of the poster or speculation about the opportunities to be expected from modern communication techniques cannot overlook the astonishing work produced by the birth of lithography. These works fulfilled, and in principle continue to fulfill, the most important demands imposed by the large format: visibility, simplicity of message, originality of forms, singularity of color scheme and intellectual clarity. The ferment which emerged around 1900 in painting, music, architecture, design and also in posters, may have contributed to the noticeably confident mood which distinguished the beginning of the machine age.

As the designer no longer executes his visual ideas manually, but rather realizes them mechanically by means of electronically-controlled cameras,

Basler
Freilichtspiele
1959
19.-31. August
im
Rosenfeldpark

Giselle

his relationship to content and expression, to form and color has changed. The whole of sensory perception has been shifted by the photographic image. It is certainly no exaggeration to say that today we stand before a situation similar to that which medieval man faced at the start of letterpress printing. The photographic way of seeing which has developed in contemporary industrial society seems to put our entire communication structure into question. Symbolic interpretation is required of an object represented photographically in black and white. However, any abstract traits disappear completely when the use of color is introduced. When we go from the black and white to the color photograph, quite certainly we have done more than merely add a broader dimension.

Color has driven photography entirely from the domain of "reading" and banished it to the realm of "viewing." The image acquires an authenticity which seems comparable to life itself. Especially the advertising artist and the advertising expert have succumbed to the temptation to simulate reality in such an exact and reliable way. The medium is too brilliant, too simple, not to be used falsely. Only a few designers began to thoroughly investigate the phenomenon of photography at the dawn of its era. El Lissitzky, Moholy-Nagy, Man Ray and later, in the 30s and 40s, Herbert Matter, Will Burtin, Herbert Bayer and others, sought in America to bring to the black and white image visual form appropriate to the medium. But too early those experiments were discontinued and the circle of people ready to pursue photographic research was too small, thus preventing the poster from being able to renew itself against the background of photography. The rapid advance of color photography made it seem untenable to question what the medium might really be about. People were already busy with the next phenomenon: the movable color image on the television screen and the videotext.

In the future, electronic advertising media will strongly compete with the poster. The poster has a chance of survival only if it recollects its most innate strength: size, clarity and simplicity. Of course, these formal necessities must be realized within the context of more complex information. This will require some effort on the part of the designer. Practically speaking, the designer of tomorrow will have to pursue research in the area of the sign. He will not be able to simply let the machine transfer a design onto the printing carrier. Reproduction techniques themselves have spread so pervasively that they can influence the content of a statement. Early lithographic posters are pioneers in the respect that they exhibit coherence between the visual idea and its reproductibility.

Armin Hofmann teaches graphic design at the Allgemeine Gewerbeschule, Basel, Switzerland, and is Director of the Yale Summer Program in Graphic Design, Brissago, Switzerland.

section
allemande
herbert boyer dorland berlin
exposition
de la société des artistes
décorateurs grand palais
14.mai-13.juillet
H.CHACHOIN IMP. PARIS 1930

Merrill C. Berman's extraordinary collection of 20th-century posters provides the core of this book and the exhibition it accompanies. As is true of all significant collections, his is the result of profound knowledge and a deep regard for the artists and designers who have created these works of graphic art. Alma Law and Merrill Berman share an interest in the Russian film poster; that common background was the basis for their conversation about collecting.

Alma Law:
How did you first become interested in collecting graphic art?

Merrill Berman:
My parents were collectors of American antiques and collecting was something I became involved with in childhood. From the age of ten or twelve I began collecting political ephemera, campaign memorabilia, political flags, tokens and buttons. I cut my teeth on campaign art, and in a sense, my later appreciation of graphic design came from an early and constant exposure to this material. It had color, typography; candidates trying to communicate to a mass audience through their posters and buttons. I pursued this interest until I went to college, and then more or less forgot about it.

When I came back to collecting, it was to collecting art, mainly contemporary art, but also post-impressionist and American abstract expressionist art. I was, for example, an early collector of works by Richard Estes, who became one of America's most renowned photorealist painters, and of paintings by Wayne Thiebaud. This was in late 1966 or 67. There were some quite nice paintings in that collection, but I didn't really get a sense of personal fulfillment from that field.

Through a combination of study and developing one's eye, and also collecting, one's taste is gradually refined, and that's what's happened to me. But it became impossible to go on, as the cost of many of these paintings had become quite prohibitive. I had important Gorkys, Pollocks and de Koonings and several Soutines. I had a Renoir, and other quite substantial pieces. Yet I didn't feel that I was doing anything more than participating in a trend that had already been well-documented and well-exhibited. There was no personal contribution beyond that of selecting a fine painting or being in a position to buy it. So in 1973 I decided to sell the collection.

In the meantime, I had started to renew my interest in graphic art. I rediscovered my own collection of political material and decided to build on that. I felt that being a pioneer in a field was more exciting and meaningful than coming into an area that was very well mined. You can contribute more to a little known field and have more personal gratification as a collector by bringing together material from the far corners of the earth, putting it into a collection, exhibiting it and making other people aware of it. This was stimulating, and it also involved some scholarship.

My own collection of political ephemera actually carried me right into graphic design. Some of the earliest examples of graphic art were the broadsides and woodcuts done in the 18th and 19th centuries for commercial and political purposes, even before the use of color lithography. There are some fantastic 19th-century pieces done in textile form and on paper for candidates like Andrew Jackson, William Henry Harrison and John Quincy Adams. There was also the European broadside, like the one I have for the Revolution of 1848, right after the overthrow of Louis Napoleon. The designers were often unknown artisans or printers, but the pieces they created really stand out because of their use of color, type and layout. Some of these artisans developed the technique of lithography, the use of stone lithography and chromolithography.

Was there any specific incident or particular poster that caused you to move into 20th-century graphic design?

It was really the 19th-century product advertising and political poster that led me into the more sophisticated 20th-century "art" poster. When I was traveling around Europe in the early 1970s, especially in France, I came across posters in flea markets and antique shops, and I met a few people who were selling posters. That was when Art Nouveau was being rediscovered, so the first posters that I was exposed to were works by Mucha, Privat-Livemont, Steinlen, Grasset, and of course, Chéret.

A lot of political advertising done between 1896 and 1908 for the campaigns of William Jennings Bryan, McKinley and Taft had used Art Nouveau graphics; some of the campaign buttons had incredible Art Nouveau designs, very much akin to the work being done at the time by Grasset, Mucha and Berthon. That's why I was able to swing over and appreciate Art Nouveau posters when I saw them in Europe.

(p. 94)
Herbert Bayer
Section Allemande
1930, lithograph
62¼ x 46⅛, 158.2 x 117.3
Collection Merrill C. Berman

German section
Exhibition of the Society of
Decorative Artists
[dates and place are listed]

Gustav Klutsis
USSR—The Shock Brigade of
World Proletariat
1931, lithograph
56½ x 40⅝, 143.7 x 103.2
Collection Merrill C. Berman

[title repeated in German, upper
right]

Then there was Art Deco. In Paris I became increasingly aware of posters by Cassandre. I also came across other material in poster form that didn't fit into obvious categories. One of the most extraordinary discoveries was a large poster by Herbert Bayer, "Section Allemande," 1930 (p. 94). It was for a decorative arts and crafts exhibition in Paris. Bayer had by that time left the Bauhaus and had his own design studio in Berlin called Dorland. "Section Allemande" was an extraordinary work because it involved things I had never seen before in posters such as a new method of typographical layout, photomontage, and the use of geometric or abstract forms.

The next thing I found was a group of Soviet political posters. There were probably thirty of them from a museum in Belgium, or perhaps they had come out of the Soviet Union. I was never really able to establish exactly where they had come from.

This, in a sense, also provided a link to your earlier interest in political ephemera?

I had always been interested in political material. I was a political science major in college and had studied the Russian political system. And so I found these posters quite fascinating. One of them, for example, which was done in 1931, incorporated photographs, a photomontage of Trotsky, Stalin and other Russian revolutionaries, including many leaders whom Stalin later purged. Other pieces dealt with the Five Year Plans; they were exciting in terms of color, type and design.

I hadn't really delved into the meaning of typography, the avant-garde or photomontage, but just the way type was used in these Russian works made them quite distinctive from the decorative poster. Most collectors at that time were interested in decorative posters, not with those with greater content. The Russian posters were distinctly non-decorative and they were trying to communicate something. You just knew that there was something special about these pieces, in their extraordinary use of color, form and typography. They obviously emanated from some major art movement.

It must have required a great deal of research and detective work to track down these obscure posters.

There's very little source material with which to educate yourself about these posters, so you feel like you're flying by the seat of your pants, and that was the exciting part of it. The more you dug around and expanded your contacts with dealers in books and with collectors, the more posters you could find that were meaningful. One would come across pockets of some of the most exciting material.

Bart van der Leck
Plantennet Delfia
1919, gouache
(maquette)
34¼ x 23⅛, 87 x 58.7
Collection Merrill C. Berman

[Last of ten designs for a poster
advertising salad oil. Never
executed.]

El Lissitzky
Russian Exhibition
1929, intaglio
49¾ x 35⅝, 126.5 x 90.5
Collection Merrill C. Berman

[The youth of Russia float above
the pavilion designed by El
Lissitzky for a Zurich
exhibition.]

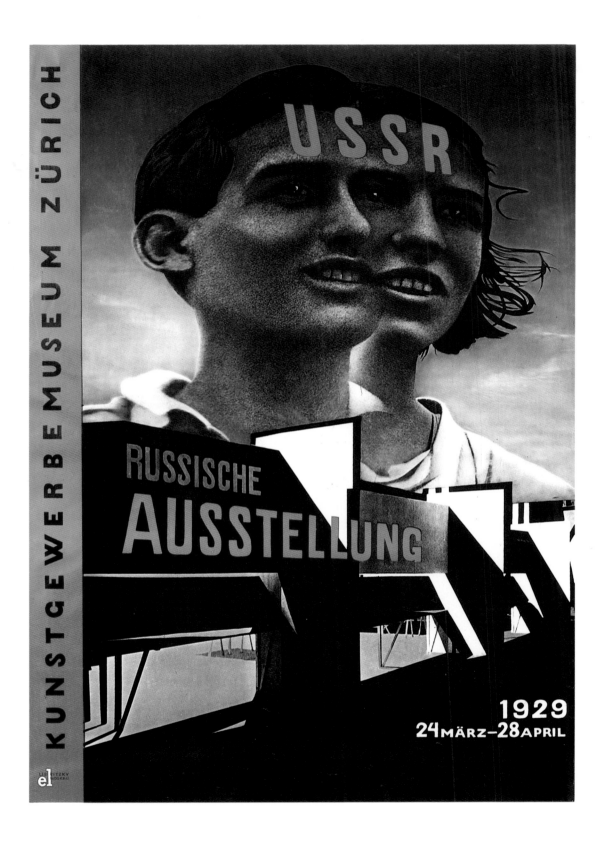

Also, it was fortunate that I met like-minded people in the field who were tilling the same soil. Robert Brown and Susan Reinhold, for example, had opened a gallery in the early 1970s devoted to antique posters. They had the German objective poster, as it has come to be called, people like Lucian Bernhard who were designing commercial graphic material in the 1900–1920 period. There were other styles that I became aware of such as the Vienna Secession, the Mackintosh group in Scotland, and the Beggarstaffs in England. There were various categories that became evident as I pursued the subject more and more. One could run across this material, but not in great quantity. There were also some great American artists, Bradley and Penfield, for example, who were making illustrations between 1896 and 1910.

Some of the posters from World War I were also very interesting, and of course there was Futurism, Dadaism and the Bauhaus. Those artists developed spectacular posters and in the process they revolutionized typography. Later I began to pick up constructivist pieces from the 1920s and De Stijl material. With the Russian material people like Arthur Cohen and his colleagues at Ex Libris, also specialists like Gail Harrison Roman, were a great help. And there are others. John Vloemans, an antiquarian bookseller in The Hague, has a tremendous appreciation of architecture and book design and of the Russian avant-garde.

How would you assess the relative influence of the various artists and movements you have discovered in the course of building your collection?

As great as some of the pioneering work coming out of the Bauhaus and De Stijl was, probably the greatest influence has come from the Russians. Russian typography was so juicy and exciting. You know, some of the theater posters for Meyerhold's theater, for example, and of course, Rodchenko and El Lissitzky, who was traveling to western Europe. He was certainly a pivotal figure. But there were many, many anonymous people doing equally incredible work. Some of them were true unsung heroes whose names we'll never know.

I think the work of the 1920s set the standard for everything that people take for granted in contemporary design, even our own commercials and television graphics. It all came out of the frenetic brilliance of the 20s. And yet, we still have not by any means plumbed the depths of the eastern European avant-garde, the Polish avant-garde, for example, and the other Slavic countries. There are so many more names, more artists, and more material that we have to see . . . from Russia and other east European countries as well.

This is evident in the most recent Polish exhibition in Paris. The work by the Blok group, for example, is fantastic, very exciting graphically. And in terms of the use of photography, they had a totally different slant from that of the Russians. The fact that these people were crossing paths with each other, and all the work they were producing was permeating mass culture through the film poster, for example, has also yet to be explored. Take, for instance, the Stenberg brothers and their film posters. These works are breathtakingly beautiful and important. I think you have to look at them again and again and you see different things each time. I think their impact on the art world is yet to be felt.

The very fact that there were so many major figures, not only artists, but literary figures and architects working in this format, suggests that this was an area of fascination for the artists themselves. Once again it shows the synthesis and the integration of all aspects of culture that was at the basis of movements like Constructivism and the Bauhaus in the 1920s. It was just not easel painting anymore. It covered all aspects of culture: book design, textiles, architecture, theater. In that sense you could say that the graphic arts really brought together many areas of artistic endeavor.

As your collection has developed—and of course, it has grown enormously in these few years—where are you today? What is the process you're going through now, a continuation of discovery, refinement?

I think the discovery process is something you can't predict, it's just something that happens. But for me, being able to bring all this material together has been a continuing mission. First of all you have to be lucky enough to come across these works and to be in a position to buy them. You have to consider their condition. Often they have to be restored. A lot of this material would have been spread to the far corners, or never been rediscovered and a lot of it might even have been destroyed. So there's the continuing process of search and discovery. A great deal still remains to be uncovered, especially in eastern Europe.

Even in Germany we're coming across unknown works as members of the avant-garde and their families die and their archives and collections and libraries become available. We're not that far away from the great figures of the 1920s, some of whom are still alive, and if not, often their heirs have material. So there's probably another twenty years of rediscovery and of putting material together from all these distant fields, the Russian avant-garde, and the western European movements. There's also ephemera— little broadsides, programs—brilliant examples of graphic design, a quarter the size of a poster.

The goal is to continue a systematic rediscovery of these materials, and to build an archive that will be valuable to people who are interested in graphic design and in the synthesis of design and all other forms of art, and that will also be helpful in giving a certain identity and profile to the artists themselves, something better than just being buried in the cobwebs where they might not have been discovered for quite a while, if ever. I think a lot remains to be done.

Lucian Bernhard
Bosch
1915, lithograph
18 x 25¼, 45.6 x 64.2
Collection Merrill C. Berman

What advice would you have for someone who is interested in collecting graphic design?

From a collector's point of view graphic design is in a very early phase. The material is important artistically, it is visually exciting, and it is still to some degree available. One of the virtues of this field is that it is an area where someone like myself can build a systematic and comprehensive collection.

On a unit basis the price of these works is low compared to other art, either graphic works of known artists, or original works, and they're probably of equal importance, and sometimes of greater importance than original artworks. Some of these posters are very rare although they were probably made in multiples. Originally many of them were totally ignored and all known copies of many works were destroyed. The basic point about posters is that almost no one has had any regard for them. Art historians and critics have had little regard for anything existing in multiple copies made for mass consumption. Also, art dealers prefer one-of-a-kind works. They can't relate to multiples unless they're numbered and signed by a famous artist. It's a prejudice that has affected the attitude of many people toward this material. They have never understood typography, anything with a message. A poster has typically been something seen in the window of a drugstore or a butcher shop. It was advertising, not art.

I think that if one started collecting painting today, one would have to have absolutely staggering resources, whereas here, for a relatively modest sum I have been able to put together a very systematic, comprehensive collection of design material (i.e. posters and ephemera) by some major figures in 20th-century art and graphic design. The fact that this was a relatively unknown and neglected area, for one reason or another, has meant that it presented a great opportunity, a great challenge.

One of the negatives about collecting is that you get frustrated. What are you really doing? Can you really accomplish anything? You can collect a few things, get a few nice examples, but can you ever really make a major contribution to the field? The exciting thing in dealing with graphic works is that one is able to pursue things as a scholar and as a collector at the same time in a comprehensive and systematic fashion. Any enduring value in collections of graphic materials will stem directly from their cultural, historical and aesthetic qualities. This will be more widely recognized as curators and other collectors participate and carry on the discovery. And in the meantime there is enormous satisfaction in rescuing and preserving many of these vital works.

**Merrill C. Berman heads
a private investment firm
in New York City.**

Plates

Ferdinand Andri
XXVI Ausstellung Secession
1906, lithograph
36⅞ x 24⅞, 93.7 x 63.2
Collection Merrill C. Berman

XXVI Secessionist Exhibition

Oskar Kokoschka
1908 Kunstschau
1908, lithograph
37¼ x 15⅜, 94.6 x 39
Collection Merrill C. Berman

1908 Art Exhibition
May–October
Vienna, No. 1 Schwarzenberg
Palace

Josef Maria Olbrich
Secession, Christus im Olymp,
Max Klinger
1899, lithograph
33 x 20¼, 83.8 x 51.4
Collection Museum of Art, The
Pennsylvania State University

Christ on Olympus

Josef Maria Olbrich
Secession
1898, lithograph
29¾ x 18⅜, 75.6 x 46.7
Courtesy Fischer Fine Art, Ltd.

To the age its art;
To art its freedom
[motto of Vienna Secessionists]
Holy Spring, Secession
Art Exhibition of the Union of
Plastic Artists of Austria
in Vienna.

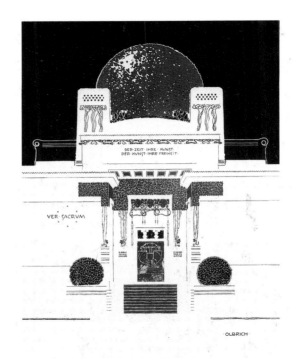

Alfred Roller
XIV Secession
1902, lithograph
36⅞ x 23⅞, 93.7 x 60.5
Collection Merrill C. Berman

Klinger, Beethoven
[Refers to a contemporary
statue of Beethoven by the
Leipzig artist Max Klinger as
displayed at the Secession,
1902. The Secession artists
transformed their building into
a temple to consecrate Klinger's
statue.]
Holy Spring, 5th year
[dates are listed]

Alfred Roller
XVI Secession
1902, lithograph
37 x 12⅛, 94 x 30.8
Collection Merrill C. Berman

Exhibition of the Union of Plastic
Artists of Austria
Holy Spring, 6th year
[dates and times are listed]

Adolf Boehm
VIII Ausstellung Secession
1900, lithograph
34 x 23¾, 86.5 x 60.2
Collection Merrill C. Berman

VIII Secessionist Exhibition

(designer unknown)
1. Ausstellung der
Jury Freien
circa 1905, lithograph
24⅞ x 35½, 63.1 x 90.3
Collection Merrill C. Berman

First Exhibition without jury
Artist's House
Brünn [City in Austrian Empire;
now Brno, in Czechoslovakia.]

Will Bradley
Victor Bicycles
1895, lithograph
40⅝ x 13⅜, 103.2 x 33.9
Collection Merrill C. Berman

Edward Penfield
Orient Cycles
circa 1896, lithograph
41½ x 27½, 105.5 x 70
Collection Merrill C. Berman

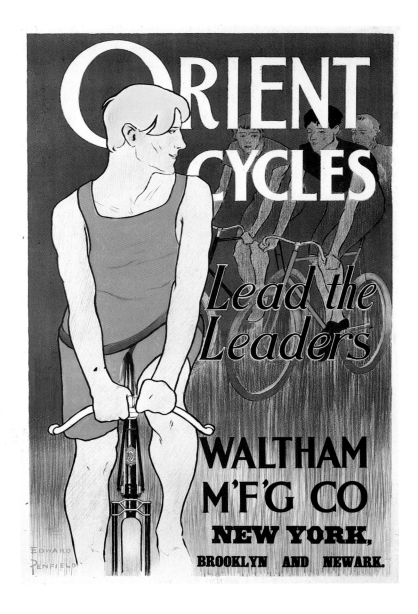

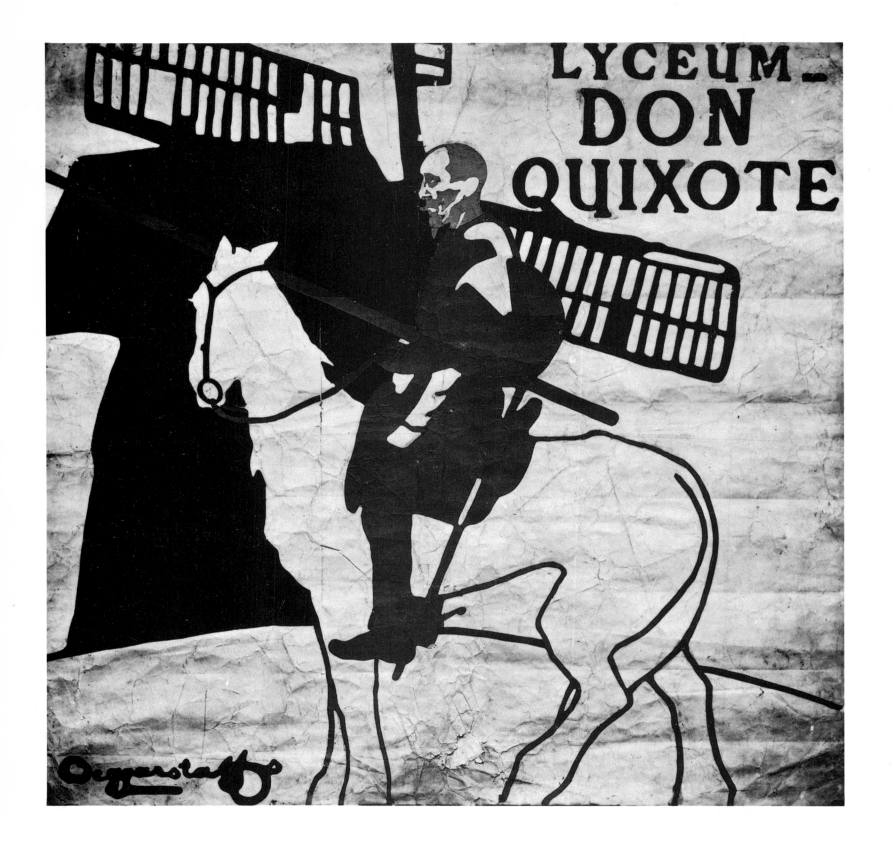

The Beggarstaffs
Don Quixote
1896, colored paper cutouts on
paper
(maquette)
76 x 77¼, 193 x 196.2
Collection Victoria and Albert
Museum
acq. no. E.1208-1927

Lucian Bernhard
Adler
1909, lithograph
27⅝ x 37⅜, 70 x 95
Collection Merrill C. Berman

Adler Works [factory]
in the vicinity of Heinrich Kleyer
Co., Zimmer Street

Otto Baumberger
PKZ
1923, lithograph
50¼ x 35½, 127.5 x 90.2
Courtesy Reinhold-Brown
Gallery

Ludwig Hohlwein
PKZ
1908, lithograph
50 x 38, 127 x 96.5
Courtesy Reinhold-Brown
Gallery

Ludwig Hohlwein
Hermann Scherrer
1908, lithograph
49 x 35½, 124.5 x 90.3
Collection The Museum of
Modern Art, New York
Gift of Peter Muller-Munk

Hermann Scherrer, breeches
maker, sporting tailor
Munich, Neuhauser Street 32

Schnackenberg

CONSÉE, MÜNCHEN.

Odeon Casino

Walter Schnackenberg
Odeon Casino
1920, lithograph
46⅜ x 34¾, 117.8 x 88.4
Collection Merrill C. Berman

Caddy
ÉTÉ
1925, lithograph
19¾ x 31½, 50.2 x 80
Collection Victoria and Albert
Museum
acq. no. E.245-1981

Summer

R · M · S · P
SOUTH AMERICAN
SERVICE
THE ROYAL MAIL STEAM PACKET CO
ATLANTIC HOUSE MOORGATE LONDON E·C·2

Frederick Charles Herrick
RMSP South American Service
1921, lithograph
39⅝ x 24¾, 100.8 x 63
Collection Merrill C. Berman

Piet Zwart
Verloop
1923, lithograph
17½ x 17½, 44.5 x 44.5
Collection Elaine Lustig Cohen

Housing Bureau Course
telephone 11577
Anna Paulowna Street 49
The Hague

VERLOOP TEL 11577 WONING BUREAU ANNA PAULOWNASTR 49 A HAAG

Alexander Rodchenko
Theater of the Revolution, *Inga*
1929, letterpress
29¾ x 41¾, 75.6 x 106
Collection The Museum of
Modern Art, New York
Gift of Jay Leyda

[Poster for the production of
Anatoly Glebov's play *Inga* at
the Moscow Theater of the
Revolution]

Director: Maksim A.
Tereshkovich
Sets and costume sketches:
Alexander Rodchenko

Alexander Rodchenko
N.E.P.
1923, lithograph
13½ x 17½, 34.3 x 44.5
Collection Elaine Lustig Cohen

[N.E.P. (New Economic Policy)
poster promoting shares in
"Dobrolet" State Merchant Air
Service]
Hear ye . . . hear
ye . . . hear ye . . .

He who isn't a stockholder in
Dobrolet is not a citizen of the
USSR
One gold ruble makes anyone a
stockholder in Dobrolet
Shares on sale at Dobrolet and
Prombank [Bank of Industry]

Stenberg brothers
Moscow Kamerny Theatre
1923, lithograph
31⅞ x 21⅞, 81 x 55.5
Collection Merrill C. Berman

[Performances in Paris,
6–23 March, 1923
Repertoire and artistic directors
are listed]

Vladimir Mayakovsky
ROSTA
1920, lithograph
24⅜ x 24⅛, 62 x 61.5
Collection Merrill C. Berman

ROSTA
The Ukranians and Russians
have a single slogan—
The landowner won't be master
over the worker!

Hannah Höch
Frühlings-Messe der
Kunstgewerbe Gruppe
circa 1925, lithograph
14⅛ x 18½, 35.9 x 46.7
Collection Merrill C. Berman

Spring Fair of the Applied Arts
Group of the German Lyceum
Club
[place and dates are listed]

Auguste Herbin
Bal de la Grande Ourse
1925, lithograph
48⅛ x 30, 122.3 x 76.3
Collection Merrill C. Berman

Ball of the Great Bear
8 May 1925
Organized by the Union of the
Russian Artists in Paris
[price and details are listed]

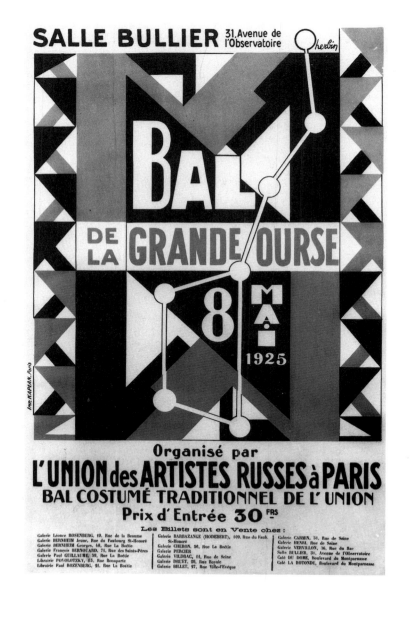

Peter Röhl
Konstruktivistische Ausstellung
1923, lithograph
36⅜ x 23¼, 92.3 x 59
Collection Merrill C. Berman

Weimar
Constructivist Exhibition
architect: Josef Zachmann
painters: M. Burchartz, W.
Dexel, Peter Röhl
[dates and place are listed]

Joost Schmidt
Ausstellung Bauhaus
1923, lithograph
27 x 19, 68.6 x 48.3
Collection Merrill C. Berman

Official Bauhaus Exhibition
opening postponed to
15 August 1923
Weimar

Henryk Berlewi
Mechano = Fakturowych
1924, gouache
(maquette)
24¾ x 19⅜, 63 x 49.2
Collection Merrill C. Berman

[Mechanical Reproduction]

Robert Delaunay and
Granovsky
soirée du cœur à barbe
1923, lithograph
35⅜ x 23⅝, 89.8 x 60
Collection Merrill C. Berman

[The heart was painted by
Delaunay, typography by
Granovsky]

Evening of the Bearded Heart
organized by Tcherez
[dates, place and times are
listed]

Tristan Tzara
Salon Dada
1921, offset lithograph
46 x 30⅛, 116.9 x 76.5
Collection Elaine Lustig Cohen

Nobody is supposed to
ignore dada
to the death
Who wants a pair of claques?
[people paid to applaud]
All in all
Dada trap Immobilization

Forget me not, please
One looks for athletes
Salon Dada
International Exposition
[dates and times are listed]

Ilia Zdanevitch
ILIAzDE
1922, lithograph
21⅝ x 18⅞, 55 x 48.1
Collection Merrill C. Berman

Eulogy by Ilia Zdanevitch,
nicknamed the Angel, about
himself, a stupid boor, coward,
traitor, idiot, scoundrel and
scabrous whore: on his
birthday, triumphantly
conceived.

(designer unknown)
Lecture by Vsevolod Meyerhold
1926, lithograph
28½ x 42⅝, 72.5 x 108.2
Collection Merrill C. Berman

[The lecture, "15 Theses for 15 Episodes," was followed by a performance of two segments of Meyerhold's 24 January 1926 production of *The Inspector General,* at the Akdrama Theatre.]

БЮРО ОБСЛУЖИВАНИЯ РАБОЧИХ ОРГАНИЗАЦИЙ при ГОСАКТЕАТРАХ.

ПОНЕДЕЛЬНИК, 24 ЯНВАРЯ   В ТЕАТРЕ **АКДРАМЫ**   **ПОНЕДЕЛЬНИК, 24 ЯНВАРЯ**

состоится

ДОКЛАД

НАРОДНОГО АРТИСТА РЕСПУБЛИКИ

ВСЕВОЛОДА

МЕЙЕРХОЛЬДА

„**15** ТЕЗИСОВ к **15** ЭПИЗОДАМ" о постановке „РЕВИЗОРА"

1) Недовольство Гоголя сценической трактовкой „Ревизора" 1836 г. - отправной пункт постановки 1926 г. 2) Увеселительный и обличительный спектакль. 3) Анекдотическая и биографическая характеристика персонажей. 4) Использование достигнутого в кино мастерами: Гриффитс, Крюзе, Кейтон, Чаплин и преодоление их приемами „шуток свойственных театру" LAZZI). Новые приемы актерской игры. 5) Разрушение легенды о гиперболизме Гоголя. 6) Текст. Выбор вариантов (Говорное). Устранение произносимых ремарок. 7) Речь. Вскрытие музыкальной структуры текста. 8) Фикция монолога. Своевременность и средства его упразднения. 9) Фикция деления на акты. Новые сценические деления - построение эпизодов. Укрепление этим путем основного стержня комедии. 10) Социальная характеристика среды Построение новых фигур. Вещественное оформление Стиль быта. 11) Музыка Размещение музыкального материала. 12) Реакция критики. 13) Генеральная аттака всеми силами малой критики и ее результат Ответ зрителя. 14) Три типа критиков: театроведы, рецензенты, как рецензенты, рецензенты вне пределов квалификации. 15) Обвинение постановки в трех смертных грехах: мистика, эротика, асоциальность. Наш ответ.

Доклад сопровождается демонстрацией диапозитивов.

АКТЕРАМИ ГОСУДАРСТВЕННОГО ТЕАТРА им. Вс. МЕЙЕРХОЛЬДА

ПРЕДСТАВЛЕНЫ БУДУТ:

ДВА ЭПИЗОДА СПЕКТАКЛЯ

РЕВИЗОР

Сценический текст (композиция вариантов) в обработке Вс. Мейерхольда и М. М. Коренева.

Эпизод 6-й **ЗА БУТЫЛКОЙ ТОЛСТОБРЮШКИ.** ■ Эпизод 10-й **ЛОБЗАЙ МЕНЯ.**

ДЕЙСТВУЮЩИЕ:

Хлестаков **Гарин.**	Марья Антоновна **Бабанова.**	Капитан **Маслацов.** ■
Анна Андреевна **Зинаида Райх.**	Заезжий офицер **Кельберер.**	

Автор спектакля — **ВСЕВОЛОД МЕЙЕРХОЛЬД.**

Режиссеры-лаборанты М. М. Коренев, Н. В. Цетнерович, Х. А. Локшина.

В ОБМЕНЕ МНЕНИЙ („СПОРЫ О РЕВИЗОРЕ") примут участие

(по алфавиту) Адонц Г. Г., Альмединген Б. А., Воскресенский С. А., Гвоздев А. А., Гутман Д. Г., проф. Державин Н., Кугель А. Р., Маширов А. И., Назаренко П. Н., Падво М. Б., Петров Н. В., Пиотровский А. И., Слонимский А. Л., Соловьев В. Н. и др.

Для членов профсоюзов билеты распределяются через Бюро Обслуживания Рабочих Организаций (БОРО) Улица Росси, № 2. Телефоны: 474-46, 107 22, 108-15, 41-45.   БИЛЕТЫ ПРОДАЮТСЯ ежедневно в кассе театра Тел. 217-60.

Начало в 7½ час. вечера.

Vasilii Ermilov
Ukrainian Artists' Exhibition
1927, woodblock
(artist's proof)
38⅝ x 26¼, 98 x 71.7
Collection Merrill C. Berman

An exhibition of Ukrainian
books and periodicals on the
10th anniversary of the October
Revolution

The House of State Industry
[dates and entrance fees are
listed]

Karel Teige
Architektury
1929, lithograph
25⅛ x 37½, 64 x 95.3
Collection Merrill C. Berman

International Exhibition of
New Architecture
Traveling exhibition of German
Werkbund and Union of
Czechoslovak Architecture
Organized by "Stavba,"
Club of Architects

[dates, place, times and
countries represented are
listed]

Anatoly Belsky
Five Minutes
1929, lithograph
42⅛ x 28½, 106.8 x 72.4
Collection Merrill C. Berman

[The film poster title, *Five Minutes*, refers to the five-minute work stoppage at the time of Lenin's interment.]

Goskinprom (Soviet) Georgia, 1929
Directors: Balagin and Zelondzhev-Shipov
Starring: L. Poltoratsky and E. Churelev

Schulz-Neudamm
Metropolis
1926, lithograph
83 x 36½, 210.9 x 92.7
Collection The Musuem of
Modern Art, New York
Gift of Universum-Film
Aktiengesellschaft

A film by Fritz Lang
with Brigitte Helm and Gustav
Fröhlich
UFA Film
Script: Thea von Harbou
Music: Gottfried Huppertz

Herbert Bayer
Ausstellung Europäisches
Kunstgewerbe
1927, lithograph
34½ x 22⅞, 87.6 x 58.2
Collection Merrill C. Berman

Exhibition of European Applied
Arts
Leipzig Grassimuseum
[dates are listed]

Georg Trump
Bielefeld
1927, photomontage with
collage
(maquette)
23⅛ x 18, 58.8 x 45.7
Collection Merrill C. Berman

Exhibition at the School of
Applied Arts
Bielefeld

(designer unknown)
Film und Foto
1929, lithograph
32½ x 22¾, 82.6 x 57.8
Collection Merrill C. Berman

Film and Photo
International Exhibition of the
German Industrial
Confederation
Stuttgart 1929
[details of places and times are
listed]

Niklaus Stoecklin
Der Buchdruck
1922, lithograph
50½ x 35¼, 128.2 x 89.3
Collection Merrill C. Berman

Book Printing
Applied Arts Museum, Basel
[dates are listed]

Niklaus Stoecklin
Schweizerische Städtebau-
Ausstellung
1928, lithograph
50¼ x 35⅝, 127.6 x 90.4
Collection Merrill C. Berman

Swiss City Building Exhibition
Zurich, Museum of Art

Vilmos Huszar
Boulevard St. Michel
1927, lithograph
14½ x 18, 36.8 x 45.6
Collection Merrill C. Berman

M. Wechsler
Children of the Storm
1926, lithograph
27½ x 42⅛, 70 x 107
Collection
Kunstgewerbemuseum der
Stadt Zürich, Museum für
Gestaltung

Leningradkino
Directors: Eduard Johanson,
Friedrich Ermler
Photographer: Naum
Aptekman
Starring: Mili Taut-Korso and
Sergei Glagolin

C. O. Müller
Der Scharlachrote Buchstabe
circa 1927, linoleum cut
46½ x 32⅝, 118 x 82.9
Collection Merrill C. Berman

The Scarlet Letter at the
Phoebus Palast Theater
Director: M. Demmel
with Lillian Gish and
Lars Hanson
[A is a possible allusion to the
Scarlet "A" worn by Hester]

C. O. Müller
Manege
circa 1927, linoleum cut
32½ x 46½, 82.5 x 118
Collection Merrill C. Berman

Manege, with Ernest van Düren
in the Phoebus Palast Theater
Director: M. Demmel

Walter Dexel
Fotografie der Gegenwart
1929, lithograph
33 x 23⅜, 83.8 x 59.4
Collection Merrill C. Berman

Exhibition of current
photography on Lake Adolf-
Mittag
Presented by the exhibition
office of the city of Magdeburg

and by the Magdeburg Union
for German Industrial Artists
[dates and times are listed]

E. McKnight Kauffer
International Aero Exhibition
1929, lithograph
30 x 45, 76.2 x 114.3
Collection Merrill C. Berman

E. McKnight Kauffer
Cheap Return Tickets
1927, lithograph
39⅞ x 24¾, 101.5 x 62.8
Collection Merrill C. Berman

E. McKnight Kauffer
Season Tickets Weekly
1928, lithograph
39⅞ x 25, 101.5 x 63.5
Collection Merrill C. Berman

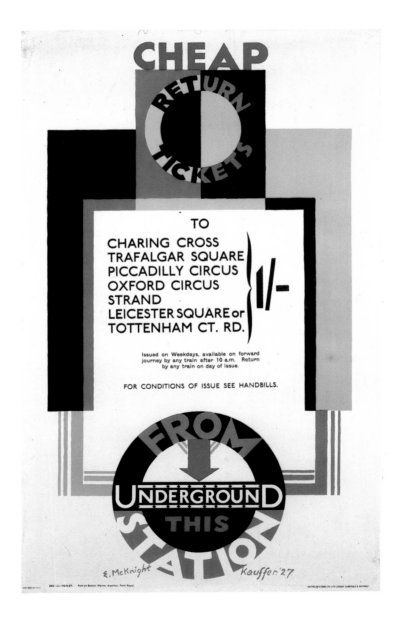

Jan Tschichold
Die Hose
1927, offset lithograph
47⅛ x 33⅛, 119.6 x 84.1
Collection Merrill C. Berman

The Panties
based on the play by Carl
Sternheim with Werner Krauss
and Jenny Jugo

Jan Tschichold
Kiki
1927, offset lithograph
48⅞ x 33¼, 124.2 x 84.5
Collection Merrill C. Berman

Jan Tschichold
Die Kameliendame
1927, offset lithograph
46⅝ x 33⅛, 118.6 x 84.1
Collection Merrill C. Berman

The Lady of the Camelias
with Norma Talmadge

Yakov Rukhlevsky
Strength and Beauty
circa 1927, lithograph
26¾ x 37, 68.2 x 94
Collection Merrill C. Berman

[One of a series of comedies
featuring Pat and Patashon.
They seem to be holding
posters.]

Nikolai Prusakov
Law of the Mountains
1927, lithograph
41 x 26⁷⁄₈, 104.3 x 68.3
Collection Merrill C. Berman

Soviet Georgia, 1927
Director: B.A. Mikhin
Cameraman: A. I. Polikevich
Starring: V. Bestaev,
I Gantarina, N. Sanov
[The above is printed on the
newspaper along with the word
"Sensation" repeated several
times.]

Ladislav Sutnar
Výstava Moderního Obchodu
1929, lithograph
17⅝ x 23⅛, 44.8 x 58.7
Collection Merrill C. Berman

Exhibition of Modern Trade
Czechoslovakia
Brno Exhibition Grounds
Exhibition of Beer Production
Exhibition of Modern Woman
[dates are listed]

Gustav Klutsis
Transportation
1929, lithograph
28¾ x 20⅛, 73.2 x 51
Collection Merrill C. Berman

Transport—one of the most
important tasks in fulfilling the
Five-Year Plan

Paul Schuitema
Zuur Werk
circa 1930, lithograph
21¾ x 15⅞, 55.2 x 40.2
Collection Merrill C. Berman

Through the action of the Dutch
Federation
7 hour week
Union of persons in public
service

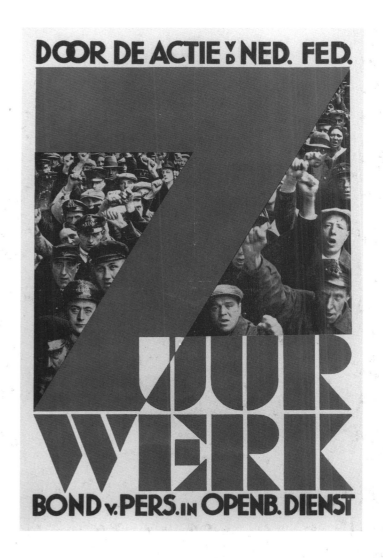

Alexei Gan
First Exhibition of
Contemporary Architecture
1927, letterpress
42½ x 27¾, 107.3 x 70.5
Collection The Museum of
Modern Art, New York
Gift of Alfred Barr

Fortunato Depero
Teatro Goldoni
Il Nuovo Teatro Futurista
1924, lithograph
55⅛ x 39⅜, 140 x 100
Collection Musei Civici di
Rovereto, Galleria Museo
Depero

Theater Goldoni
Friday 25 January 1924
The New Futurist Theater

Hendrikus Wijdeveld
Frank Lloyd Wright
1931, lithograph
30¼ x 19¼, 76.8 x 48.8
Collection Arthur A. and Elaine
Lustig Cohen

Architecture of Frank Lloyd
Wright
First European exhibition of the
works of American architect
Frank Lloyd Wright in the City

Museum of Amsterdam
[dates and other details are
listed]

Hendrikus Wijdeveld
Economisch-Historische
1929, lithograph
25½ x 19¾, 64.8 x 50
Collection Merrill C. Berman

Exhibition of International
Economic History
Pictures, Miniatures, Tapestries,
Documents, Models, Graphics
City Museum of Amsterdam
[dates are listed]

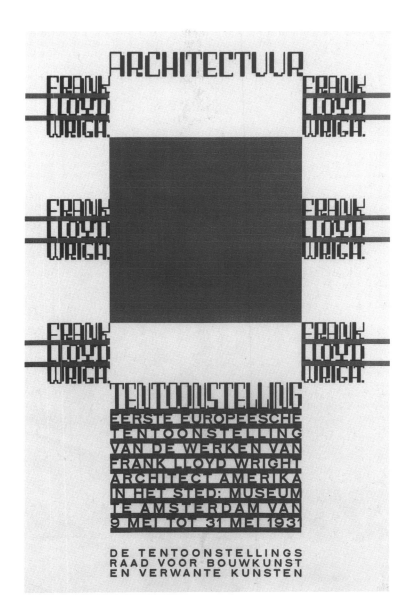

Paul Renner
Fachschulen Bayerns
1928, lithograph
50 x 35⅜, 127 x 90
Collection
Kunstgewerbemuseum der
Stadt Zürich,
Museum für Gestaltung

Technical Schools of Applied
Arts of Bavaria
Exhibition at Applied Arts
Museum, Zurich

Jean Arp and Walter Cyliax
abstrakte und surrealistische
malerei und plastik
1929, lithograph
50½ x 35⅝, 128.3 x 90.5
Collection Merrill C. Berman

Abstract and surrealist painting
and sculpture
Exhibition at the Zurich
Museum,
6 October–3 November 1929

Max Burchartz
Tanz Festspiele
1928, offset lithograph
35¼ x 32¾, 90 x 83.2
Collection The Museum of
Modern Art, New York,
Special purchase

Dance festivals for the Second
German Dance Congress,
Essen, 1928.

Alexandre Alexeieff
Dine on the L.N.E.R.
1928, intaglio
40⅛ x 50¼, 102 x 127.7
Collection Merrill C. Berman

Alexandre Alexeieff
The Night Scotsman
1932, lithograph
40 x 50, 101.6 x 127
Collection Victoria and Albert
Museum
acq. no. E.453-1932

THE NIGHT SCOTSMAN
Leaves King's Cross nightly at 10.25.

PUBLISHED BY THE LONDON & NORTH EASTERN RAILWAY.   PRINTED IN ENGLAND.   WATERLOW & SONS LTD LONDON, DUNSTABLE & WATFORD.

Theo Ballmer
Neues Bauen
1928, lithograph
50 x 35½, 127 x 90.1
Collection Merrill C. Berman

Applied Arts Museum
New Construction
Traveling exhibition of the
German Industrial
Confederation

Theo Ballmer
Bureau Bâle
1928, lithograph
50¼ x 35¾, 127.5 x 90.7
Collection Merrill C. Berman

Industrial exhibition of the Basel
Department in the Palace of the
Swiss Fair.

Theo Ballmer
100 Jahre Lichtbild
1927, lithograph
50¼ x 35¾, 127.5 x 90.2
Courtesy Reinhold-Brown
Gallery

100 Years of the Photograph
[dates and times are listed]
Exhibition Applied Arts
Museum, Basel

Jean Carlu
Theatre Pigalle
1929, lithograph
60¾ x 39½, 154.1 x 100.3
Collection Merrill C. Berman

Lights, machinery

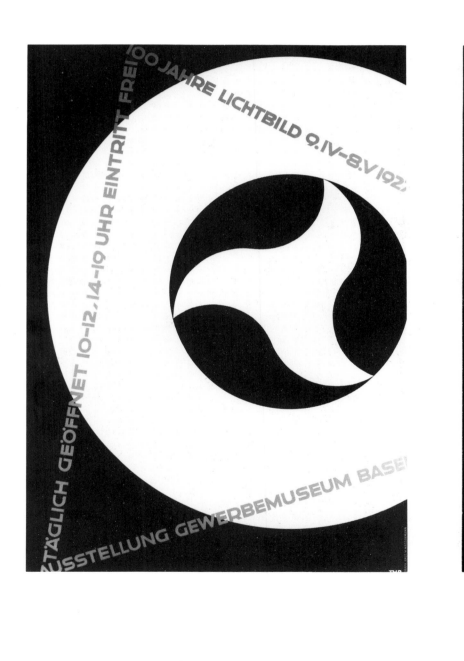

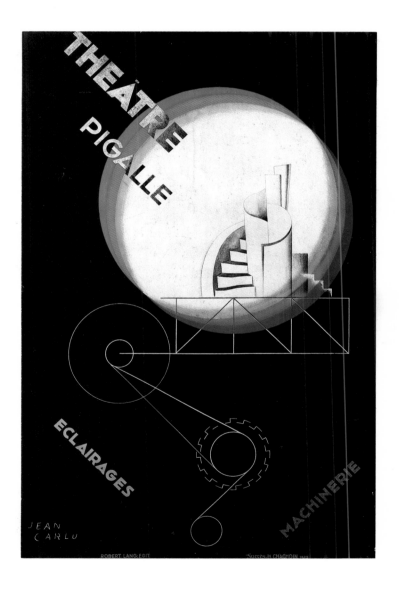

Walter Dexel
Verwende stets nur Gas
1924, letterpress
20¼ x 26½, 51.5 x 67.3
Collection Merrill C. Berman

Always use only gas for cooking,
baking, heating and lighting
because it is practical, clean and
cheap. Saves work, time and
money.
Information and exhibition in
Municipal Gas Works

Mart Stam
Internationale Architectuur
Tentoonstelling
1928, letterpress
39⅝ x 26, 100.6 x 66.2
Collection Merrill C. Berman

International Architecture
Exhibition
50 architects of international
fame with 298 designs of
objective "fantasyless"
architecture organized by the

Building Union in Rotterdam in
the restaurant De la Paix
Coolsingel 103, Rotterdam

Kurt Schwitters
dammerstock
1929, lithograph
32⅝ x 22⅞, 83 x 58
Collection Merrill C. Berman

Dammerstock [a housing
settlement]
Exhibition in Karlsruhe of the
utility home, under the direction
of Walter Gropius
[dates are listed]

Ernst Keller
Presseball
1932, lithograph
50⅜ x 35¾, 128 x 90.9
Collection Merrill C. Berman

Zurich Press Ball
Hotel Baur au Lac
19 November 1932
[list of collaborators]

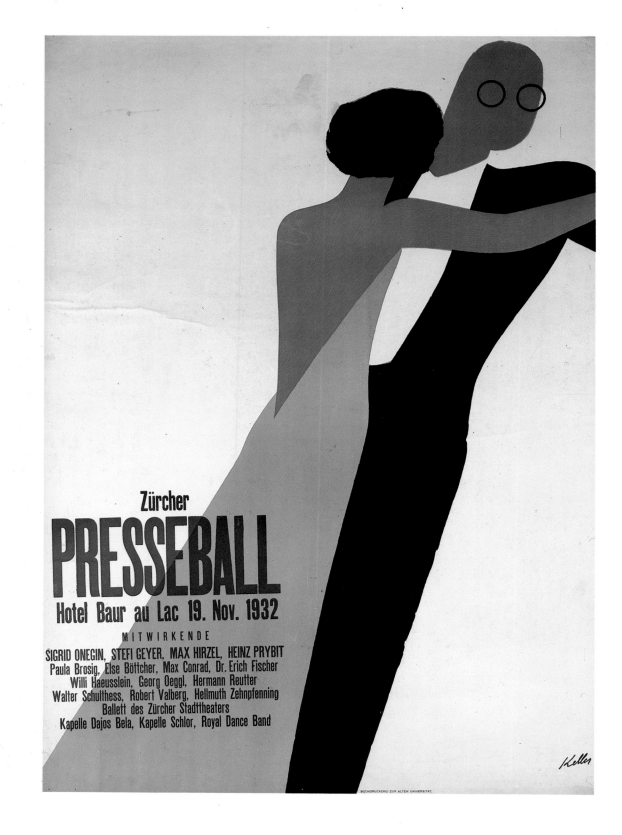

Wilhelm Deffke
Manoli Gold
1929, lithograph
47¼ x 35½, 120 x 90.3
Collection Merrill C. Berman

Horace Taylor
The Royal Mail Line
circa 1925, lithograph
38⅜ x 25, 97.6 x 63.5
Collection Merrill C. Berman

A. M. Cassandre
Au Bucheron
1923, lithograph
59 x 157½, 150 x 400
Collection Susan J. Pack

[Au Bucheron was a large
furniture store at 10 rue de
Rivoli, Paris.]

A. M. Cassandre
La Route Bleue
1929, lithograph
39 x 24¼, 99.1 x 61.6
Collection Merrill C. Berman

Blue Route

A. M. Cassandre
Nicolas
1935, lithograph
94½ x 126, 240 x 320
Collection Merrill C. Berman

[Advertisement for a wine
merchant.]

A. M. Cassandre
Étoile du Nord
1927, lithograph
41⅜ x 29½, 105 x 75
Collection Susan J. Pack

North Star

A. M. Cassandre
Dr. Charpy
1930, lithograph
39⅜ x 24⁷⁄₁₆, 100 x 62
Collection Susan J. Pack

[Dr. Charpy cosmetics.]

A. M. Cassandre
L.M.S. Bestway
1928, lithograph
39⅞ x 49¾, 101.2 x 127.7
Collection Merrill C. Berman

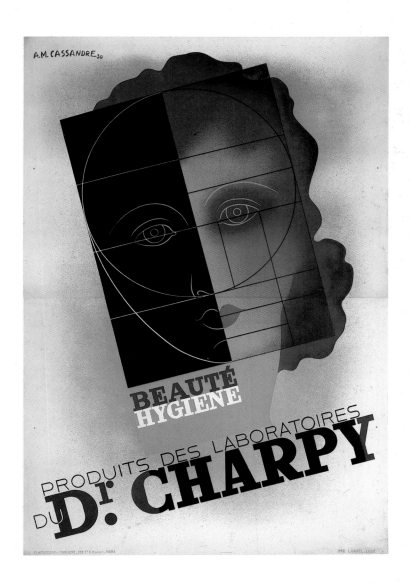

A. M. Cassandre
Dubonnet
1932, lithograph
17⅞ x 35⅜, 45.3 x 89.9
Collection Merrill C. Berman

Dubo = doubt
Du bon = of some good
Dubonnet = the product is
identified and the glass and the
man are filled

A. M. Cassandre
Triplex
1930, lithograph
47¼ x 31⅛, 120 x 79.1
Collection Merrill C. Berman

[Manufacturer of safety glass
for trucks.]

A.M. Cassandre
L'Atlantique
1931, lithograph
39¾ x 25, 101 x 63.5
Collection Merrill C. Berman

[A passenger ship en route to
South America.]

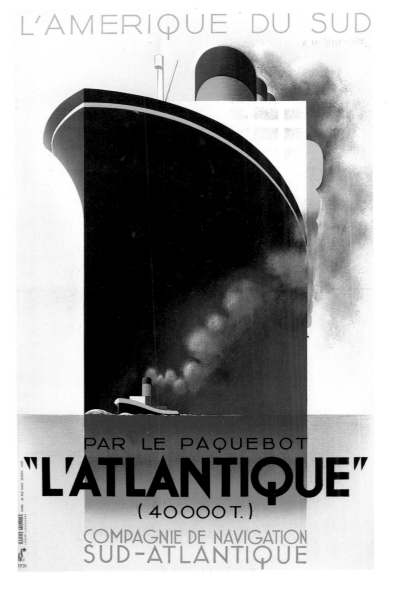

A. M. Cassandre
Nord Express
1927, lithograph
41⅜ x 29½, 105 x 75
Collection Susan J. Pack

Northern Express

Jean Carlu
Union des artistes modernes
1931, lithograph
21¾ x 15¼, 55.3 x 38.7
Collection Merrill C. Berman

Union of Modern Artists
Exhibition at the Galleries
Georges Petit

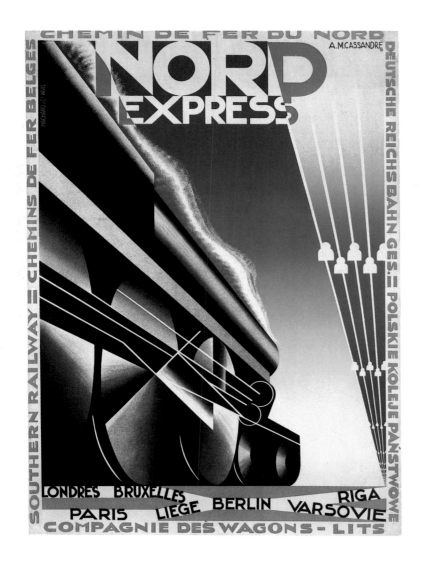

Gustav Klutsis
USSR—The Shock Brigade of
World Proletariat
1931, lithograph in two parts
(top) 29 x 40⅜, 73.7 x 102.6
(bottom) 28¾ x 40¾,
73.1 x 103.6
Collection Merrill C. Berman

Proletarians of all countries,
defend your socialist homeland
[words along the flagpole]

(designer unknown)
[probably Ilya Shlepianov who
designed the production
advertised on the poster]
Moscow Realistic Theater
1929, lithograph
21⅝ x 28⅝, 54.9 x 72.7
Collection Merrill C. Berman

[Announcement of the opening
of the 1929–30 season at the
Moscow Realistic Theater
(former Fourth Studio of the

Moscow Art Theatre).]

10–14 October: *North-East* by
D. Shcheglov. Director: Vasilii
F. Fedorov. Artist: Ilya
Shlepianov. Balletmaster: L. I.
Lukin.

Matinee, 13 October: *The Third
Shift* by Yu. Bolotov. Director:
A. M. Mikhailov. Artist: N. N.
Obrucheva and R. V. Raspopov.
Music: A. A. Golubentsev.

Helmut Kurtz
Neue Hauswirtschaft
1930, lithograph
50½ x 32¼, 128.1 x 81.9
Collection Merrill C. Berman

Exhibition of New
Home Economics
Applied Arts Museum, Zurich

John Heartfield
Das letzte Stück Brot
1932, lithograph
37¾ x 28½, 96 x 72.3
Collection Merrill C. Berman

Capitalism robs you of the last
piece of bread.
Fight for yourselves and your
children!
Vote Communist!
Vote Thälmann!

Man Ray
Keeps London Going
1932, lithograph
39¹¹⁄₁₆ x 24½, 100.8 x 62
Collection The Museum of
Modern Art, New York
Gift of Bernard Davis

Paul Schuitema
A.N.V.V. reemdelingenverkeer
1932, lithograph
39¼ x 25½, 99.7 x 64.8
Collection Merrill C. Berman

Buy A.N.V.V. Stamps
Support the work of the General
Dutch Union for Foreign Travel

Walter Käch
Ausstellung
Der neue Schulbau
1932, lithograph
50 x 35¼, 127 x 89.5
Collection Merrill C. Berman

Exhibition
The New School Construction
Museum of Arts and Crafts,
Winterthur

Max Bill
Ariadne
1931, lithograph
25⅜ x 36¾, 64.3 x 91
Collection Merrill C. Berman

City Theater matinee
24 April 10:45
dance studio wulff, basel
[Includes notice of
postponement of a ballet by

Satie and Picabia and a
statement of aesthetics in small
type.]

Xanti Schawinsky
Illy Caffè
1934, lithograph
55⅛ x 39½, 140.2 x 100.2
Collection Merrill C. Berman

Tom Purvis
East Coast Resorts
1925, lithograph
40 x 50⅜, 101.6 x 127.9
Collection Victoria and Albert
Museum
acq. no. E.745-1925

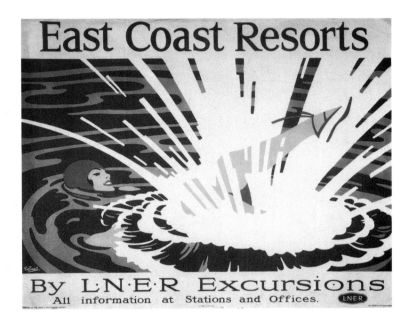

Tom Purvis
East Coast by L.N.E.R.
1925, lithograph
40⅛ x 50, 101.9 x 127
Collection Victoria and Albert
Museum
acq. no. E.744-1925

Charles Loupot
St. Raphael Quinquina
1938, lithograph in two parts
47⅝ x 63, 121 x 160
Collection Susan J. Pack

[St. Raphael aperitif]

Niklaus Stoecklin
Valvo
1931, lithograph
50⅛ x 35½, 127.5 x 90.2
Courtesy Reinhold-Brown
Gallery

Jean Carlu
America's answer! Production
1942, lithograph
30 x 40, 76.1 x 101.5
Collection The Museum of
Modern Art, New York
Gift of the Office for Emergency
Management

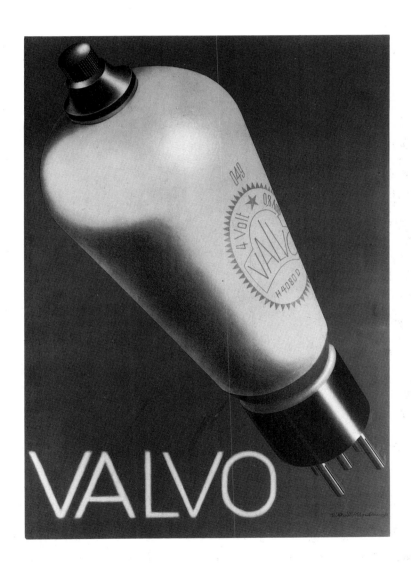

Xanti Schawinsky
Olivetti
1934, lithograph
20½ x 13½, 52 x 34.3
Collection W. Michael Sheehe

J. S. Anderson
You can be sure of Shell
1935, lithograph
30 x 45⅛, 76.1 x 114.5
Collection Merrill C. Berman

Herbert Matter
Bila till Schweiz
1935, intaglio
39⅞ x 25¼, 101.5 x 64.2
Collection Merrill C. Berman

Motor to Switzerland

Hermann Eidenbenz
Grafa International
1936, lithograph
50¼ x 35⅝, 127.5 x 90.4
Collection Merrill C. Berman

Graphic Technical Exhibition by
Grafa International,
Basel, in the Model Fair
Building
[dates and times are listed]

Ernst Keller
Wählt Liste 4
1935, linoleum cut
52⅛ x 38⅞, 132.4 x 98.7
Collection Merrill C. Berman

Vote List 4

Numa Rick
USA Baut
1946, lithograph
50¼ x 35⅝, 127.8 x 90.5
Collection Merrill C. Berman

USA Builds

Karl Koehler, Victor Ancona
This is the Enemy
1942, offset lithograph
34¼ x 23¾, 84.5 x 60.4
Collection The Museum of
Modern Art, New York,
Purchase

Marcel Duchamp
DADA 1916–1923
1953, lithograph
38 x 25, 96.5 x 63.5
Courtesy Reinhold-Brown
Gallery

Josef Müller-Brockmann
19. volkskonzert
1959, linoleum cut and
letterpress
50⅜ x 35⅝, 127.8 x 90.5
Courtesy Reinhold-Brown
Gallery

19th Public Concert
Musica Viva under the direction
of Hans Rosbaud
[dates, times and program are
listed]

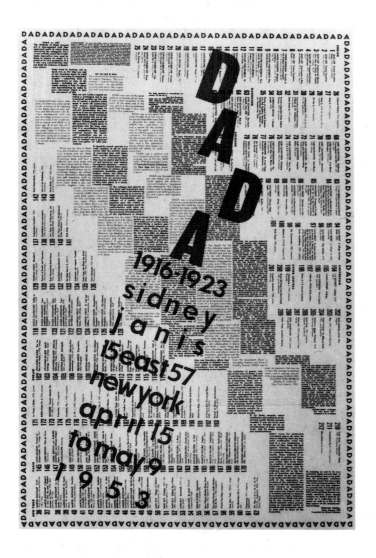

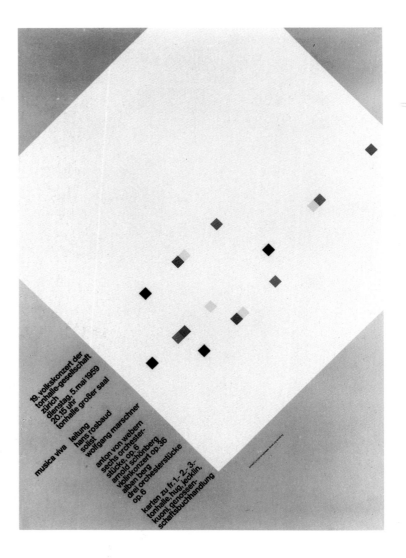

Josef Müller-Brockmann
beethoven
1955, offset lithograph
50¼ x 35½, 127.5 x 90.3
Courtesy Reinhold-Brown
Gallery

Concert at the Tonhalle, Zurich
[dates, times and program are
listed]

Massimo Vignelli
XXXII Biennale/Internazionale/
D'arte Venezia/
32B.20 Giugno/18 ottobre 1964
1964, offset lithograph
38⅛ x 27⅛, 96.7 x 69
Collection The Museum of
Modern Art, New York
Gift of the designer

Pieter Brattinga
De man achter de vormgeving
van de p.t.t.
1960, offset lithograph
25 x 14¾, 63.3 x 37.6
Collection The Museum of
Modern Art, New York
Gift of de Jong and Co.
Hilversum/Baarn, Holland

An exhibition of the work of
Chris de Moor,
the man behind the design of
the post office.

Emil Ruder
die Zeitung
1958, letterpress
50¼ x 36½, 127.6 x 90.1
Collection Thomas Strong

The Newspaper
Gewerbemuseum, Basel
[dates and times are listed]

Gewerbemuseum Basel
Ausstellung «die Zeitung»
9. April bis 18. Mai 1958
Geöffnet
werktags 10-12 und 14-18
sonntags 10-12 und 14-17
Eintritt frei

die
Zeitung

Ben Vautier
ART TOTAL
1967, letterpress
23⅜ x 16⅝, 59.3 x 42
Courtesy Reinhold-Brown
Gallery

Total Art
Action, Poetry, Fluxus
[and many other poems
announcing the program]

Hansjörg Mayer
herman de vries
1967, letterpress
27½ x 27½, 69.8 x 69.8
Courtesy Reinhold-Brown
Gallery

Books, graphics and objects
in the gallery of the publishing
house of Hansjörg Mayer
[dates and times are listed]

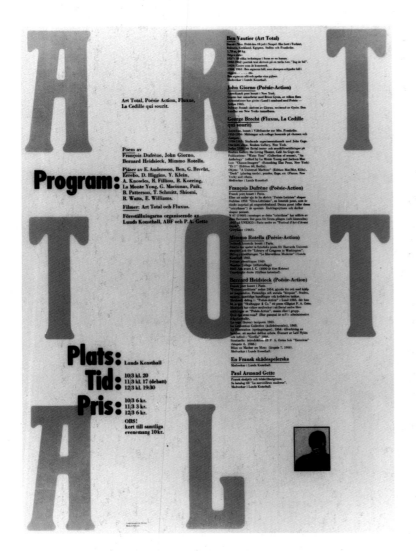

Paul Rand
Alfred North Whitehead
1965, offset lithograph
(designer's proof)
35¹¹⁄₁₆ x 22, 90.7 x 55.9
Collection the designer

with the sense of sight,
the idea communicates the emotion...
Alfred North Whitehead

Tadanori Yokoo
Having Reached/A climax at the
age of 29/I was Dead
1965, silkscreen
43 x 31⅛, 109.2 x 79.1
Collection The Museum of
Modern Art, New York
Gift of the designer

Tadanori Yokoo
The City and Design/
Isamu Kurita
1966, silkscreen
41 x 29½, 104.1 x 75
Collection The Museum of
Modern Art, New York
Gift of the designer

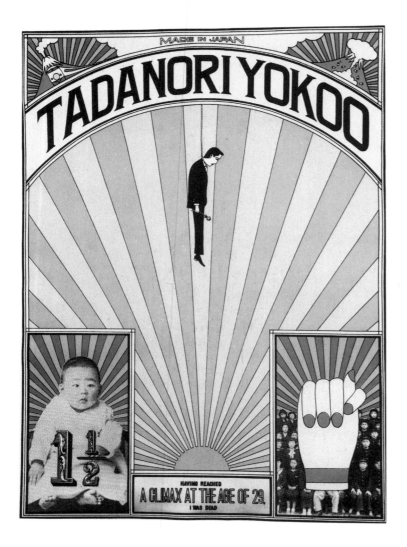

Shigeo Fukuda
Keio Department Store
1975, silkscreen
40⅝ x 20¼, 103.1 x 51.4
Collection Walker Art Center
Art Center Acquisition Fund

Shigeo Fukuda
Mt. Fuji
1976, silkscreen
40¾ x 28⅞, 103.5 x 72.8
Collection Walker Art Center
Art Center Acquisition Fund

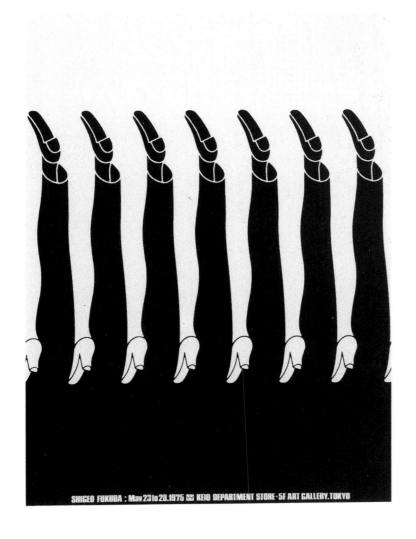

Ivan Chermayeff
Winston Churchill: The Wilderness Years
1982, lithograph
45¹⁵⁄₁₆ x 29¹⁵⁄₁₆, 116.7 x 76.1
Collection the designer

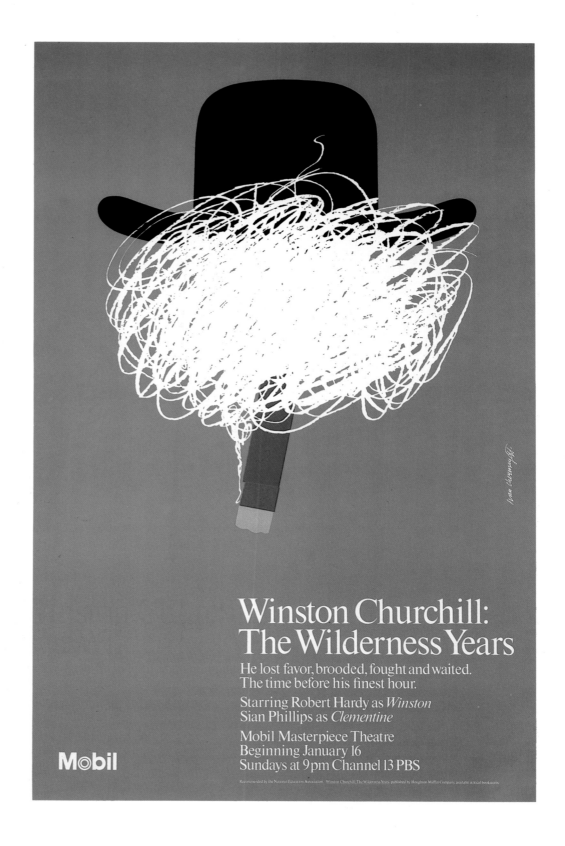

Ivan Chermayeff
International Design
Conference, Aspen
1973, lithograph
36 x 24, 91.6 x 61
Collection the designer

Seymour Chwast
End Bad Breath
1967, woodcut
37½ x 24½, 95.3 x 62.2
Collection Seymour Chwast/
Pushpin Lubalin Peckolick, Inc.

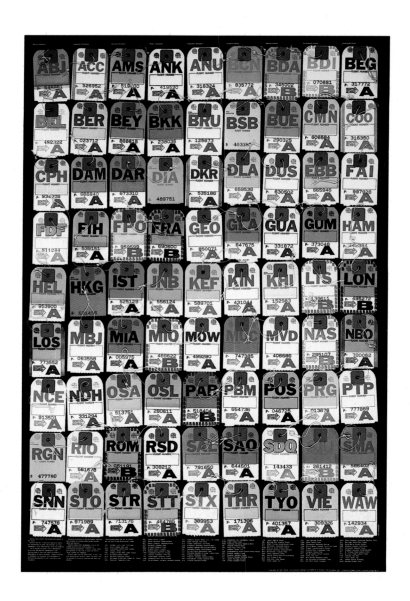

Rambow + Lienemeyer
Charlie Chaplin *Gold Rausch*
1962, silkscreen
47¹³⁄₁₆ x 33⅛, 121.4 x 84.1
Collection the designers

[This poster for *The Gold Rush*
was designed for a round kiosk;
the figure moves as the observer
circles it.]

Rambow, Lienemeyer,
van de Sand
S. Fischer
1976, offset lithograph
46¹¹⁄₁₆ x 33¹⁄₁₆, 118.7 x 83.9
Collection the designers

[A series of posters (three of
eleven) for the Frankfurt
publisher S. Fischer-Verlag.]

Rambow, Lienemeyer,
van de Sand
S. Fischer
1979, silkscreen
46¾ x 33⅟₁₆, 118.8 x 84
Collection the designers

Rambow, Lienemeyer,
van de Sand
S. Fischer
1979, offset lithograph
46¹¹⁄₁₆ x 33⅟₁₆, 118.7 x 83.9
Collection the designers

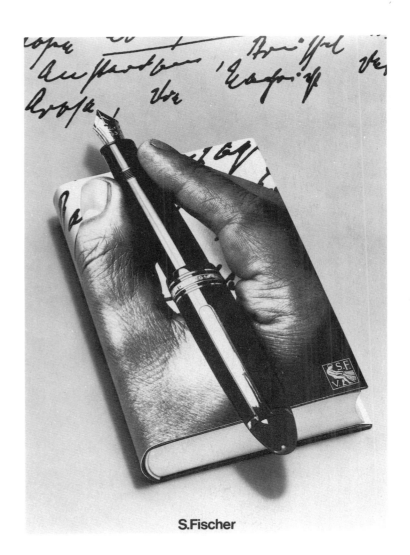

Daniel Friedman
Yale Symphony Orchestra
1973, silkscreen
25⅝ x 19⅞, 65.2 x 55
Collection the designer

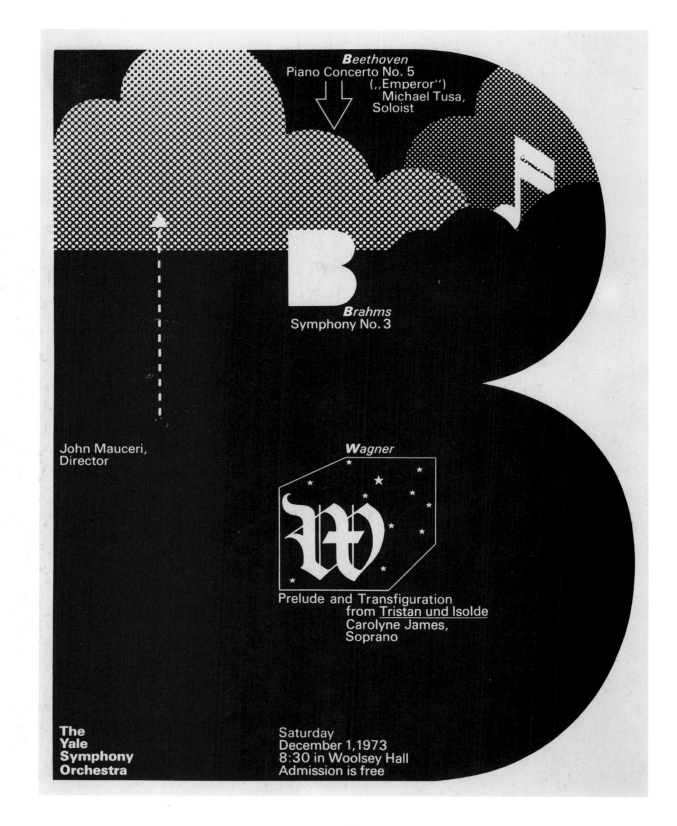

April Greiman and
Jayme Odgers
Academy of Television Arts &
Sciences Student Television
Awards
1981, offset lithograph
36 x 24, 91.3 x 61.2
Collection April Greiman

April Greiman
Your Turn, My Turn
1983, offset lithograph (with 3D
glasses)
36 x 24⅛, 91.3 x 61.2
Collection the designer

Wolfgang Weingart
The Swiss Poster 1900–1983
1983, offset lithograph
50¼ x 36½, 127.6 x 90.1
Collection the designer

Inge Druckrey
Yale Symphony Orchestra
1979, offset lithograph
23½ x 31½, 60 x 80
Collection the designer

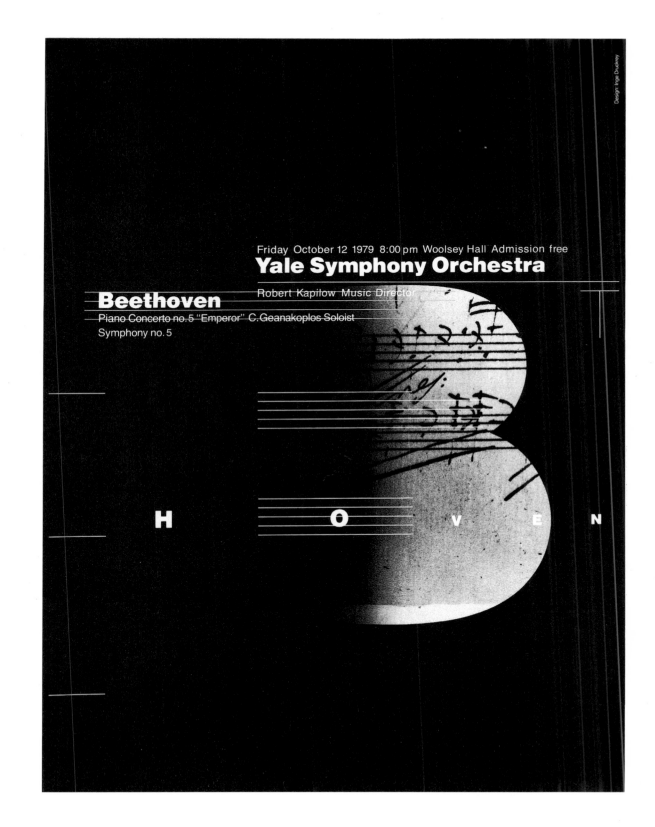

Biographies

Alexandre Alexeieff (1901–1982)
was born in Russia, but little is known about his childhood. After a career as a naval cadet he enrolled at the school of oriental languages in Paris. From 1922 to 1925 he became involved with the design of stage sets and costumes, an interest that may have developed from his studies with Serge Soudeikine, a stage designer. It is unclear whether Alexeieff ever received professional art training but he exhibited a talent for painting and advertising design. He is best known, however, for his work with film animation. In 1931 he and his wife, Claire Parker, invented a method for making animated cartoons by pushing illuminated pins into a screen. The pinboard process was employed in *A Night on Bald Mountain,* Alexeieff's first film, and later he applied the technique to book illustration.

J. S. Anderson (dates unknown)

Ferdinand Andri (1871–1956)
was an Austrian painter and graphic artist born in Waidhofen an der Ybbs. He studied at the Vienna Academy and in Karlsruhe. Andri joined the Vienna Secession in 1899 and remained a member until 1909. From 1905 to 1906 he was President of the Artists' Union. He was Professor at the Academy in Vienna from 1919 to 1939, and during this time also served as Pro-rector of the Academy from 1923 to 1926 and President of the Governing Body of the Academy in 1938–39. His poster for the twenty-sixth exhibition of the Secession demonstrates the approach of the Austrian Art Nouveau, which, influenced by the work of Charles Rennie Mackintosh, imposed a geometric order upon organic forms.

Jean (Hans) Arp (1887–1966)
was a founder of the Zurich dada group in 1916. In addition to his contributions as abstract sculptor and painter he wrote both poetry and prose. In 1926 Arp settled in Paris with his wife, the artist Sophie Taeuber-Arp. With Theo van Doesburg, the couple designed the Café Aubette, the great De Stijl interior in Strasbourg, the city of Arp's birth. Walter Cyliax (1899–1945), who was Arp's typographer-collaborator on the poster included here, was born in Leipzig, Germany and died in Vienna, Austria.

Theo Ballmer (1902–1965)
a native of Lausanne, Switzerland, began formal design training in high school. Following employment with a printing firm in Lausanne, he traveled to Zurich (circa 1923) and became a student at the Kunstgewerbeschule under Ernst Keller. In the late 1920s he spent an indefinite period of time at the Dessau Bauhaus under the tutelage of Paul Klee, Walter Gropius and Hans Meyer. In his poster designs of 1928 Ballmer combined De Stijl principles and an ordered grid to create harmonious visual forms. He became an instructor at the Basel Allgemeine Gewerbeschule in 1931 and taught there for more than thirty years.

Otto Baumberger (1889–1961)
was one of three or four artist/designers who helped establish a Swiss school of graphic design in the early part of this century. Except for periods of schooling in Munich, Paris and London, it appears that he spent most of his lifetime in the city of his birth, Zurich. Baumberger was apprenticed to a lithographer there and in 1914 he began an affiliation with the Wolfensberger printing firm. After World War I he became involved in stage decoration and by 1920 was designing sets for Max Reinhardt's Deutsches Theater in Berlin, and for the Stadttheater and Schauspielhaus in Zurich. In 1923 Baumberger designed an elegant poster for Burger-Kehl & Co., the renowned men's clothier founded in 1881 by Paul Kehl of Zurich using the familiar PKZ label as the focus for his design.

Herbert Bayer (b. 1900)
in Haag, Austria, lives in California. He began his career apprenticing in architectural studios in Linz and Darmstadt where he was concerned with the decorative arts and graphic design as well as architecture. Bayer began his rise to prominence as one of the first generation of Bauhaus students from 1921 to 1923. From 1925 to 1928 he taught typography and advertising at the Dessau Bauhaus where he was a leader in the revolution taking place in these fields. He replaced the tendency toward decorative compositions with ordered and economical means, designed a sans-serif alphabet, and championed the exclusive use of lowercase type which gave Bauhaus publications a unique appearance. His graphic design of the late 1920s and 1930s was also influential because of its integration of typography and photography. Bayer continued his career in New York from 1938 to 1948. From 1946 to 1976 he served as design consultant and architect to the Aspen Institute of Humanistic Studies, and from 1956 to 1967 was Chairman of the Department of Design of Container Corporation of America. Bayer has continued to participate in various design and architecture projects.

The Beggarstaffs (James Pryde, 1869–1941, and William Nicholson, 1872–1949)
Pryde was born in Edinburgh. He was a student at the Royal Scottish Academy School of the Arts and later went to Paris where he studied under Bouguereau. When he returned to London he met Nicholson who was engaged to Pryde's sister. Nicholson was born at Newark-on-Trent where he received his earliest artistic education before traveling to Paris to study at the Académie Julian from 1889 to 1890. He returned to England and enrolled at Sir Hubert von Herkomer's school in Bushey where he met Mabel Pryde. His marriage in 1893 also marks the beginning of the collaboration of the brothers-in-law. They began designing posters in response to a competition and called themselves the "Beggarstaffs" after seeing the name on a sack—because it seemed such a "good hearty, old English name." Both Pryde and Nicholson admired the work of Lautrec, but they developed a style all their own. They designed spare compositions composed of large flat masses of color in simple silhouettes, with clear divisions between areas of positive and negative space. These were conceived by using paper cutouts. Their aesthetic success was not matched by commercial success. Their poster depicting the British Beefeater was rejected by many clients unwilling to be represented through such a radical style before it was finally purchased by *Harper's* magazine. The period of the Beggarstaff collaboration was therefore brief, lasting only until 1899. Each artist went on to pursue independent careers in painting, printmaking and theatrical design.

Peter Behrens (1868–1940)
began his career as a painter but after 1890 was attracted to design and the crafts under the influence of the teachings of William Morris. In this period he designed typefaces and produced Art Nouveau graphics. These pursuits led to an interest in the problems of industrial design. In 1903 he was appointed Director of the Düsseldorf School of Art. In 1907 Behrens received an epoch-making appointment when he was named coordinator of design for A.E.G., the German General Electric Company. Behrens was also important as a teacher of a generation of architects that included Walter Gropius, Le Corbusier and Mies van der Rohe.

Anatoly Belsky (1896–1970)
was born in Moscow, where he studied at the Stroganov School from 1908 to 1917 and at the Vkhutemas from 1917 to 1921. After establishing himself as a set designer, he turned to making film posters in the second half of the 1920s. He was also involved with designs for various exhibitions including the Soviet pavilion at a 1928 exhibition in Philadelphia. In the late 1950s Belsky began painting landscapes of the region around Moscow.

Henryk Berlewi (1894–1967)
spent his childhood years in Poland, having been born in Warsaw, and as an adolescent enrolled at the Académie des Beaux-Arts in Antwerp in a traditional course of study. In 1911–12 he was introduced to Cubism at the École des Beaux-Arts in Paris. By 1922 Berlewi was at work in Berlin experimenting with the mechanization of painting and graphic design, where he began elaborating his theory of mechano-faktura (mechanical reproduction), eliminating any three-dimensional aspects from his work by mathematically placing geometric forms on a ground and using only black, white and red. A move to Paris in 1927 coincided with a change in style, to figurative painting, but Berlewi returned to his mechano-faktura compositions after World War II.

Lucian Bernhard (1883–1972)
was born in Vienna. He studied at the Munich Academy but was essentially self-taught as a designer. In Berlin in 1905 he began to design posters influenced by the Beggarstaffs, particularly their use of rounded, serif letters. Bernhard's approach to poster design, like the goods he advertised, was essentially functional in that it eliminated any superfluous elements. His posters focused on an illustration of the advertised article which loomed large in the picture. This was supplemented only by the manufacturer's name in large, clear lettering. Bernhard was especially interested in the design of typefaces and has thirty-six to his credit. In Berlin in 1920 Bernhard became the first professor of poster design at the Royal Academy. He cooperated in the establishment of the German magazine, *Das Plakat*, later renamed *Gebrauchsgraphik*. In 1923 he settled in the United States and held classes at the Art Students League and at New York University. He was co-founder of the design firm Contempora, with Rockwell Kent, Paul Poiret and Bruno Paul.

Max Bill (b. 1908)
is a Swiss painter, sculptor and graphic designer. He studied at the Zurich Kunstgewerbeschule from 1924 to 1927, and at the Bauhaus, Dessau, from 1927 to 1929. Bill then returned to Zurich where he played a major role in the emergence of a constructivist ideal in Swiss graphic design of the 1930s. In 1931 he had embraced the concept of "concrete art," a term proposed by Theo van Doesburg in 1930 to describe a universal art of absolute clarity. Bill expressed this aesthetic in work that utilized grids, geometric progressions and mathematical formulas. His 1931 poster for the ballet *Ariadne* reflects an early influence of dada design that is absent from his mature work.

Adolf Boehm (1861–1927)
was an Austrian graphic artist born in Vienna. He studied at Vienna's Academy of Creative Arts and was a member of the Vienna Secession from its founding in 1897 to 1905. Beginning in 1900 he taught at the School of Art for Women and Girls in Vienna. His most significant works were his graphic designs for *Ver Sacrum*, a Secessionist publication, but he also worked in stained glass and designed a large stained-glass window for Otto Wagner's villa, near Vienna, in 1900.

Will Bradley (1868–1962)
began his career at twelve as a printer's devil for a Michigan newspaper. His mother had moved there after the death of his father, a Boston cartoonist, in 1874. In 1887 he moved to Chicago to accept a position as a designer; he was completely self-taught. In 1894 Bradley's book and theater posters and a series of covers for *The Inland Printer* and *The Chap Book* marked the beginning of Art Nouveau in America. His style is characterized by sinuous line and areas of flat color, reminiscent of Aubrey Beardsley's style. In 1895 he opened the Wayside Press in Springfield, Massachusetts where he began publication of *Bradley, His Book*, a monthly arts periodical for which he was editor, artist, critic, designer, printer and publisher in one. After the turn of the century Bradley became a consultant to American Type Founders, designing type and ornaments. His interest in layout and design prompted his acceptance of the position of Art Editor for *Collier's Magazine* in 1907. In 1920 he was appointed art and typography supervisor for Hearst publications and films.

Pieter Brattinga (b. 1931)
in Hilversum, the Netherlands, received practical training in Leiden and London and had courses in drawing and art history in Paris. From 1960 to 1964 he was Professor and Chairman of the Visual Communications Department of Pratt Institute, New York, and has also lectured at Yale University. He worked as Director of Design for Steendrukkerij De Jong and Company, Hilversum, from 1951 to 1974, for whom he edited the Quadrat Prints, a series of printed experiments in graphic design, literature, architecture and music. Brattinga coauthored with Dick Dooijes *A History of the Dutch Poster*, published in 1968. He is senior partner of Form Mediation International, in Amsterdam, where he has designed exhibition posters and installations for the Kröller-Müller Museum, Otterlo, since 1960 and postage stamps for the Netherlands Post Office since 1970.

Max Burchartz (1887–1961)
studied in Düsseldorf, Munich and Berlin from 1906 to 1908. After World War I he lived in Hanover where he established contact with Kurt Schwitters and El Lissitzky, and in Weimar where he met Theo van Doesburg, Paul Klee and Wassily Kandinsky. He founded the agency Werbebau in Bochum, Germany in the 1920s where he wrote a number of pamphlets addressing problems of advertising and graphic design. Burchartz was thus an early disseminator of modern advertising principles and is particularly well-known for the use of photography in his designs. In 1926 he joined the staff of the Folkswagschule in Essen from which he was dismissed in 1933; he returned in 1949. Burchartz later worked as an industrial designer.

Caddy (dates unknown)

Jean Carlu (b. 1900)
at Bonnières-sur-Seine into a family of architects, began training in architecture, but after a 1918 accident in which he lost his right arm, he turned his attention entirely toward graphic design. From 1918 to 1923 Carlu was fascinated with Cubism and, along with Cassandre, introduced a geometrical treatment of forms based on the cubist style into French advertising art. His posters were simple and concentrated, brief in text, and made use of symbolism rather than realism. He called for a formal approach to poster design that would analyze the emotional value of line, color and composition rather than focus on representational or anecdotal illustration. This formalism united with a manner of execution that recalls the exactness of scientific engineering. Carlu was in America when Paris fell in 1940. He stayed to work for the Office of War Information and produced the first United States defense poster in 1941. From 1945 to 1953 he worked for a number of American firms and planned a French educational and commercial exhibition in the U.S. In 1953 he returned to France where he continued to design posters until he retired in 1974.

A. M. Cassandre (1901–1968)
was a pseudonym adopted by Adolph Jean Marie Mouron who was born to French parents in the Ukrainian city of Kharkov. He came to Paris in 1918 where he studied at the Académie Julian, painting in the style of Cézanne. The artist began making posters in 1923, which he signed "A.M. Cassandre." His avant-garde graphic designs are significant for their introduction of the aesthetics of 20th-century painting to the field of commercial design. The influence of the collages of Braque and Picasso is apparent in *L'Intransigeant,* 1925, in the fragmentation of the newspaper's name. "Étoile du Nord," "L.M.S. Bestway" and "Wagon-Bar" also reflect Cassandre's debt to cubist, purist and machine art. There is a restrained, almost monochromatic use of color, geometric abstraction, superimposed imagery and dynamic lines suggesting speed. These create a feeling of modern technology combined with the romance of travel.

In 1930 Cassandre founded the Alliance Graphique, with Charles Loupot and Maurice Moyrand. He began to design typefaces at this time and in 1934–35 he operated his own art school. His posters from this period are based on his style of the 1920s but also explore new directions. The dynamic arcs in the background of his colorful "Nicolas" poster of 1935 resemble the Orphism of Robert Delaunay. The Museum of Modern Art organized an exhibition of Cassandre's work in 1936 and the designer made a number of trips to the U.S. between that year and 1939, and at that time he produced work for several American firms.

Ivan Chermayeff (b. 1932)
attended Harvard University and the Institute of Design, Illinois Institute of Technology in the early 1950s, and later graduated from Yale University, School of Art. In 1957 he was a co-founder of Brownjohn, Chermayeff & Geismar, a design office that was reorganized in 1960 as Chermayeff & Geismar Associates (graphic and exhibition designers). Both Ivan Chermayeff and Thomas Geismar are partners in the office of Cambridge Seven Associates, an architectural and multi-disciplinary design firm in Cambridge, Massachusetts in which Chermayeff's brother, Peter is an architect. He has served on the Board of Directors for the International Design Conference, Aspen, Colorado, since 1967 and is on the Board of Directors of The Museum of Modern Art, New York.

Seymour Chwast (b. 1931)
is a 1951 graduate of the Cooper Union in New York, and was a founding partner of the celebrated Push Pin Studios. He is now a principal of Pushpin Lubalin Peckolick, Inc. His designs and illustrations have been used for magazines, posters, packaging, advertising, animated films, corporate and environmental graphics, record covers and books. He has designed and illustrated more than a dozen children's books, and was a founder of the Push Pin Press. He has received many design awards, including the St. Gauden's Medal from Cooper Union, and he was also elected to the New York Art Directors' Hall of Fame.

Austin Cooper (1890–1964)
studied at the Cardiff School of Art, Abroath, from 1906 to 1910 when he moved to London. There he studied at the City and Guilds School, Kensington. He worked for a brief period in Canada (where he was born) as a commercial artist before war service brought him back to Europe. He resettled in London in 1922 where he worked as a poster designer for L.N.E.R. (London and North Eastern Railway), the Royal Mail Line, the Empire Marketing Board and the London Underground. His 1933 poster for the British industrial art exhibition demonstrates his flexibility in adopting a style appropriate to the subject of the design. It is not typical of his more familiar pictorial style but depends entirely on bold typographical elements to create the effect of industrial modernity. Cooper was principal of the Reimann School of Commercial and Industrial Art from 1936 to 1940. In 1938 his book *Making a Poster* was published.

Wilhelm Deffke (birthdate unknown–1950)
was a German graphic designer. In the 1920s he had a studio in Berlin where he designed trademarks, posters and other graphic work for corporations and publishing houses. He later became Director of the Magdeburg Arts and Crafts School. Through his graphic design, his Berlin studio, and his position at Magdeburg, Deffke trained many in the next generation of modernist designers, including the Swiss Hermann Eidenbenz, who worked in Deffke's studio and later joined him on the staff at Magdeburg.

Alexander Deineka (1899–1969)
was born at Kursk, in Russia. He attended the Vkhutemas, a polytechnic established in 1918, from 1921 to 1925. Both German Expressionism and Surrealism influenced his work but during the early 1930s he became one of the most authoritative interpreters of Socialist Realism. From 1930 to 1934 he worked primarily in poster design, and the Revolution provided him with his themes. His 1931 poster "Transforming Moscow" depicts a modern utopia, reflecting revolutionary Russia's experiments in town planning. Deineka also produced book and magazine illustrations and was celebrated for his paintings, sculpture and mosaics.

Robert Delaunay (1885–1941)
was born in Paris and trained as a decorative and commercial painter. In 1906 he developed an interest in the color theories of Eugene Chevreul and in Neo-Impressionism which led to his own explorations of color and the development of Orphism, also known as Simultanisme. Color, light and movement were the central concerns of his painting. In the early 1920s Delaunay was friendly with a circle of artists associated with Paris dada. His wife, Sonia Delaunay-Terk, designed the costumes for the notorious 1923 production of Tzara's *Le Coeur à Gaz,* part of the festivities of the dada "soirée du coeur à barbe," for which Robert Delaunay provided the poster. The typography was designed by Granovksy using entirely lowercase form.

Fortunato Depero (1892–1960)
was a leading member of the second generation of futurists that appeared after World War I. He gained prominence as a painter, but like many other futurists, Depero turned his attention to the theater. In 1917 he was hired by Diaghilev to work for the Ballets Russes, and Depero designed costumes and decor for Stravinsky's *Rossignol*. His *Balli Plastici,* marionette ballets that incorporated music, color, light and mechanisms, were performed in Rome in 1918. Depero attempted to update futurist themes and techniques in his 1950 "Manifesto on Nuclear Painting and Plastics." Although born in Italy, Depero was an Austrian citizen, and there is a museum devoted to his work in Rovereto, Italy.

Walter Dexel (1890–1973)
studied art history in his native Munich. In 1916 he moved to Jena where he directed exhibitions at Jena's Art Union until 1928. Dexel painted in a constructivist style but was especially concerned with commercial art and typography. He designed advertisements, posters and worked to develop lighting for the outdoor display of signs and advertisements. From 1919 to 1925 he had a number of contacts at the Bauhaus, and from 1921 to 1923 was close to Theo van Doesburg. His own design excludes pictorialism. Type was combined with straight lines and geometric forms in dynamic asymmetrical compositions. In 1927 Dexel organized an Art Union exhibition, *New Advertising,* which was one of the earliest attempts to survey the developments taking place in 20th-century commercial design. Dexel taught at the School of Arts and Crafts in Magdeburg from 1928 to 1935. From 1936 to 1942 he was Professor at the State College of Art Education in Berlin-Schöneberg.

Inge Druckrey (b. 1941)
received a state diploma in graphic design from the Kunstgewerbeschule in Basel, Switzerland in 1965. She also studied art history and languages at Basel University. She is currently a Visiting Professor of Design at Yale University and has taught at the Philadelphia College of Art, the Kunstgewerbeschule, Krefeld, Germany and the Kansas City Art Institute. While teaching full-time since 1966 Druckrey has done free-lance work for both European and American clients, among them the Yale School of Music, Yale Symphony, the University Museum, University of Pennsylvania, Ganter Brewery in Germany and the Antiken Museum in Basel.

Marcel Duchamp (1887–1968)
went to Paris from his native Blainville in 1903, and studied a short while at the Académie Julian. He first exhibited at the Salon des Indépendents in 1909 and associated with Apollinaire and artists of the cubist movement. Duchamp arrived in New York in 1915 where he established himself as the leading exponent of dada. He outraged the public with his art, anti-art antics as he sought to destroy traditional concepts of aesthetic beauty. In 1923 Duchamp publicly abandoned artistic endeavors, although he continued to make works shown only after his death. His 1953 exhibition poster is a rare example of his graphic design. It reflects the constructivist precision that he utilized in the creation of his dada drawings of *The Virgin and the Bride* and his *Large Glass* of 1915 to 1923, in its clear, legible type organized on a diagonal axis.

Hermann Eidenbenz (b. 1902)
in Cannanore, India of Swiss parents, received his earliest training from 1919 to 1922 at the Art Institut Orell Füssli. He continued his studies with Ernst Keller at the Zurich Kunstgewerbeschule until 1923. From 1926 to 1932 he taught lettering and advertising art at the Arts and Crafts School in Magdeburg, Germany. He returned to Basel, Switzerland in 1932 where with his brothers he formed the Eidenbenz Studios in which he was active until 1953. He designed the ten and twenty Swiss bank notes during this time. From 1953 to 1956 he headed the graphic design department of the Werkkunstschule in Brunswick, Germany. After 1955 he continued to practice as an advertising consultant. Eidenbenz was influential in establishing the foundations of contemporary Swiss graphic design.

Vasilii Ermilov (1894–1968)
began art instruction at an early age in his native Russia, attending the School of Decorative Arts in Kharkov from 1905 to 1909. From 1910–11 he was a pupil at the Kharkov Art School and in private studios. By 1913 he was a student at the Moscow Institute of Painting, Sculpture and Architecture, and during this time in Moscow he met the cubo-futurists Burliuk and Mayakovsky, leading figures of the Russian avant-garde. In 1917 Ermilov returned to Kharkov, his style and ideology in harmony with the principles of the movement that would be defined by 1921 as Constructivism. First known as "production-art," Constructivism dealt with the problem of uniting art and society and Ermilov began to take an active role in changing the world by creating art for the masses. In 1919–20 he designed and produced agitprop posters and murals, and painted trains with simple images intended to convey messages of the Revolution to outlying areas of Russia.

Daniel Friedman (b. 1945)
graduated in 1967 from Carnegie Institute of Technology, Pittsburgh, Pennsylvania with a BFA degree, studied at the Hochschule für Gestaltung in Ulm, West Germany and at the Allgemeine Gewerbeschule in Basel. In 1970 he returned to the U.S. and joined the faculty of Yale University as an Assistant Professor in the Graduate School of Art. From 1972 to 1975 he was Assistant Professor in the School of Visual Arts, State University of New York at Purchase. Since 1975 he has lived and worked in New York City as a designer and artist.

Shigeo Fukuda (b. 1932)
in Tokyo, graduated in 1956 from Tokyo National University of Fine Arts and Music with a degree in design. Since then he has worked primarily as a free-lance designer. Fukuda's work is at the same time original, penetrating, satirical and often humorous, frequently employing a single bold image, as in his series of serigraphs on the iconic Mt. Fuji, which is immediately recognizable yet surrealistic in its scale and juxtaposition with other images. Fukuda has received numerous awards, including the gold prize in the Warsaw International Biennial of Posters, 1972, and second prize at the 9th Brno Biennial of Graphic Art in Czechoslovakia, 1980. In 1982 he was a Visiting Instructor of graphic design in the Graduate School of Art, Yale University.

Alexei Gan (1893–1940)
was, in all probability, born in Russia, but details about his early life and academic studies are unavailable. Gan became a radical spokesman for the avant-garde and was a member, perhaps co-founder, of the First Working Group of Constructivists. In 1922 he published a book that attempted to define the constructivist ideology. Gan was also a designer of architectural projects and a member of the Association of Contemporary Architects. He was art director of the group's journal, *Sovremennaya Arkhitektura* (Contemporary Architecture), and he helped organize the First Exhibition of Contemporary Architecture held in Moscow in 1927. Gan's interests extended to typography, and his poster for the exhibition indicates his characteristic use of space and extreme variations of type size. Gan also designed film posters during the 1920s and his work was shown in the First Film Posters Exhibition in Moscow, 1925.

Pierre Gauchat (1902–1956)
studied with Ernst Keller at the Kunstgewerbeschule in Zurich, and then at the Munich Kunstgewerbeschule. By 1923 he had returned to Zurich, the city of his birth, to study printing techniques at Art Institut Orell Füssli. From 1925 to 1944 he taught at the Zurich Kunstgewerbeschule and worked as a free-lance designer and illustrator, producing everything from books and tapestries to marionettes. Frequently he received advertising poster commissions and his "Bally" (1935) is typical of Gauchat's clarity of style that continues in the powerful tradition initiated by Lucian Bernhard in the early 1900s.

April Greiman (b. 1948)
is a graduate of the Kansas City Art Institute where she received a BFA. Greiman then studied at the Basel Allgemeine Gewerbeschule in 1971 with Armin Hofmann. For the next five years she lived in New York and Connecticut, taught at the Philadelphia College of Art, and designed on a free-lance basis for such clients as the Architects Collaborative and Anspach Grossman Portugal. Emilio Ambasz at The Museum of Modern Art in New York commissioned Greiman to design the catalogue and graphics for the taxi project, a 1976 exhibition of entries to a competition for the design and fabrication of a non-polluting, reasonably priced taxi. Greiman relocated in Los Angeles in 1976 and introduced the West Coast to her unique style—a combination of Swiss training under designers Hofmann and Weingart and a playful breaking of the rules. Exaggerated letterspacing, floating geometric shapes and eccentric yet cheerful colors are her hallmarks. Since 1982 she has been head of the design program at the California Institute of the Arts.

John Heartfield (1891–1968)
was born Helmut Herzfeld in Berlin. He grew up in Switzerland and then in Austrian foster homes. Helmut and his brother Weiland settled in Wiesbaden, Germany in 1905 where he was apprenticed to a bookseller, and later worked in a painter's studio. He began his studies at Munich's Kunstgewerbeschule in 1909 and continued them in Berlin's in 1913. In 1916 he changed his name to John Heartfield in response to an anti-British hate campaign. Heartfield and his brother formed the Malik Verlag publishing house in 1917. In 1919 he founded the Berlin dada group with Weiland and the painter George Grosz. In 1918 Heartfield joined the German Communist Party for which he produced posters and literature until 1933. His designs for that organization are such succinct expressions of its cause that Heartfield will always be associated with it. Heartfield is also associated with the photomontage technique of which he was a creator and an acknowledged master.

Auguste Herbin (1882–1960)
was born at Quiery, near Cambrai in France. He studied at the École des Beaux-Arts in Lille from 1900 to 1902 and afterwards moved to Paris where he worked first under the influence of the impressionists and post-impressionists and later came under the influence of the cubists. His own cubist structure gradually developed into completely abstract compositions around 1917. He briefly returned to objective painting in the 1920s but devoted the rest of his career to geometrical abstraction and to pursuing his own research into color theory. His compositions were completely flat with basic geometrical shapes in pure color. He was a founder of the Abstraction-Création Association in 1931. In 1949 he wrote *L'art non-figuratif et non-objectif* which set down the theory of his later works. He was Director of the Salon des Réalités Nouvelles until 1955.

Frederick Charles Herrick (1887–1970)
was born at Mountsorrel, Leicestershire, England. He studied at the Leicester College of Arts and Crafts and at the Royal College of Art where he won the Royal Exhibition Prize in 1908 and a traveling scholarship in 1912. After Herrick served in World War I, he designed posters for the Baynard Press from 1919 to 1926. In 1925 Herrick had the only British poster in the Exposition des Arts Décoratifs in Paris, for which he received the Grand Prix. His style has been likened to that of E. McKnight Kauffer and, like Kauffer, Herrick was often commissioned by the London Underground. He taught at the Royal College of Art and the Brighton College of Art.

Hannah Höch (1889–1978)
was born Johanna Höch in Gotha at Thuringen. In 1912 she enrolled in Berlin's School of Decorative Art. In 1915 she met Raoul Hausmann and in 1918 they both joined the Berlin dada group. Höch experimented with abstract paintings and collages from 1915 to 1918 and, together with Hausmann, was an early experimenter with photomontage. In 1922 Höch broke with Hausmann and the Berlin dada group, continuing in collaboration with Kurt Schwitters and Jean Arp on several projects from 1922 to 1925. In 1939 Nazism forced her retirement from the art scene, although not from her work. After the War Höch's work was shown in European exhibitions and her contributions to early 20th-century modernism were belatedly acknowledged.

Armin Hofmann (b. 1920)
is a native of Winterthur, Switzerland. He lives in Basel where he has taught graphic design at the Allegemeine Gewerbeschule since 1947. He trained at the Zurich Kunstgewerbeschule and has worked as a lithographer as well as a graphic designer. In 1956 Hofmann lectured at the International Design Conference in Aspen, and he has spoken on educational problems before design associations and at institutions in both the U.S. and Europe. He teaches six weeks of every year at the School of Art, Yale University, and since 1980 has been Director of the Yale Summer Program in Graphic Design, Brissago, Switzerland.

Ludwig Hohlwein (1874–1949)
was born in Wiesbaden and studied architecture in Munich where he gradually developed an interest in graphic design. He was thirty before he focused his talents on the poster and was completely self-taught as a graphic artist. He broke from Art Nouveau finding inspiration in the work of the Beggarstaffs. His early style is characterized by the use of brilliant colors, masterfully combined, and emphatically flat, bold patterns as in his 1907 poster for Hermann Scherrer, a men's clothier, and his 1908 poster for PKZ clothing. Although his approach was illustrative, it did not focus on the advertised object so much as create a context for the object full of associations which appealed to the viewer. After World War I his posters became more painterly and he combined bold shapes with more naturalistic imagery. Hohlwein designed propaganda posters for the National Socialist German Workers' Party. His style became hard and tight, reflecting Germany's cultural atmosphere in that period.

Vilmos Huszar (1884–1960)
was a student in Munich at the turn of the century. In Germany he developed an interest in applied art and graphic design, and in the early 1900s Huszar returned to his native city, Budapest, to enter the School of Applied Arts. In 1905 he moved to Holland and some years later became involved with Theo van Doesburg and De Stijl. The lettering of Huszar's cover design for the first issue of *De Stijl* magazine, 1917, reflects a close relationship to one of his own paintings of the same year in which figures of skaters become tiny horizontal and vertical rectangles. Huszar collaborated with Piet Zwart and Bart van der Leck, among others, on interior design and exhibition stands for a furniture company headed by Cornelis Bruynzeel. Huszar designed a full-page advertisement for Bruynzeel that appeared in the first six issues of

De Stijl. His association with De Stijl ended in 1923 and Huszar returned to figurative painting. However, as late as 1929 he designed a typographic poster for the Exhibition of Contemporary Industrial Arts utilizing the diagonal composition of late De Stijl.

Marcel Janco (b. 1895)
studied painting in Bucharest where he was born, and in 1912 edited the newspaper *Simboiul* with fellow Rumanians Tristan Tzara and Ion Vinea. He studied architecture from 1915 to 1916 in Zurich where he developed an interest in cubist painting. Janco played an integral part in the foundation of Zurich dada. He was charged with making posters, decorations and costumes for events at the Cabaret Voltaire and designed dada posters and newspapers with Tzara and Richard Huelsenbeck in wood and linoleum cuts. Janco's poster for the first dada exhibition of 1917 is a rather tame example of dada typographical design. Nonetheless, it reflects dada's defiance of conventions in the freely drawn letters which refuse absolute discipline and create a feeling of unrepressed, spontaneous energy, establishing a tradition for the typographic poster demonstrating that type could convey a range of emotions.

Walter Käch (1901–1970)
was a Swiss graphic designer who studied at the Kunstgewerbeschule in Zurich and at the Kunstgewerbeschule in Munich. From 1925 to 1929 Käch taught graphic design and linoleum-cut printing in Zurich at the Kunstgewerbeschule. He worked as a graphic designer from 1929 to 1940, returning to the art school at Zurich in 1940 where he taught typography and calligraphy until 1967. His books *Lettering,* 1949, and *Rhythm and Proportion in Lettering,* 1956, present his theory of structure and proportion in letters based on the golden section. Käch had a strong interest in the history of lettering and studied pre-Trajan and catacomb inscriptions. His 1932 exhibition poster, however, used a strictly 20th-century vocabulary. Its bold sans-serif type and the strong diagonal structure reflect Bauhaus design principles.

E. McKnight Kauffer (1890–1954)
was born in Great Falls, Montana. He began formal art studies at the Mark Hopkins Institute in San Francisco, and in 1913 spent six months at the Chicago Art Institute. While he was a student in Chicago Kauffer saw the infamous Armory Show which made an indelible impression on him. He decided to study in Europe and traveled to Paris by way of Munich, where he saw the elegant posters of Ludwig Hohlwein. His studies were cut short by the onset of the First World War, and he moved to London in 1914. In 1915 Kauffer received his first commission from the London Underground, the company for which he was to produce his most celebrated posters for the next twenty-five years. His early works reflect the influence of Cubism and the English vorticist movement. Kauffer was, in fact, involved in a short-lived attempt to revive Vorticism, the Group X of 1920. Consistent characteristics are his simplification of form, bold and legible composition, and symbolic imagery used to convey the essence of his subject matter. The 1930s marked the height of Kauffer's success, when his posters were common sights in the "subterranean picture galleries" of the London "Tube." This exposure is significant, for through it Kauffer's work familiarized a large public with the conventions of modern painting. The Museum of Modern Art, New York, held a one-man show of Kauffer's work in 1937. The outbreak of World War II prompted Kauffer's permanent return to the U.S. in 1940.

Ernst Keller (1891–1968)
seems to be unanimously hailed as the progenitor of the Swiss graphic design movement. He was born in Aarau, and worked for a time as a lithographic draftsman. Keller became fascinated with typography between 1912 and 1914 while a student in Leipzig, and in 1918 he joined the faculty of the Zurich Kunstgewerbeschule where he transformed a course for advertising draftsmanship into a complete training program in design and typography. During nearly four decades of teaching Keller exerted a lasting influence on design trends in Switzerland. His own work encompassed poster design (which he often hand lettered), and sculpture. Keller's posters are the antithesis of those produced by members of the Jugendstil. He advocated a return to legibility and simplicity of design in poster art as well as a unique solution for each design problem.

Gustav Klutsis (1895–1944)
was born in Latvia and attended the Riga Art Institute between 1913 and 1915, then continued his art education in Petrograd at the School of the Society for the Encouragement of the Arts. By 1918 he was studying in Moscow at Svomas (Free State Art Studios). Reorganized in late 1920, Svomas became Vkhutemas and Klutsis studied under Kasimir Malevich and Antoine Pevsner at Vkhutemas where the philosophy of education was similar in some respects to that of the Bauhaus in Weimar. By the mid-20s Klutsis had begun to commit himself to designing art to educate the masses. In 1928 Klutsis was one of the founding members of October, a group of artists dedicated to serving the needs of the proletariat, the peasant leaders and national groups in the far corners of the Soviet Union. October's scope extended to architecture, photography, film, even to festivals, and during the early 1930s Klutsis was one of the key producers of posters reflecting the group's aims. His mastery of photomontage is especially apparent in the posters that herald the proletariat as defenders of the socialist society. October was forced to disband in 1932 by a Communist Party decree, and by 1938 Klutsis had challenged the ruling Communist Party too boldly with his avant-garde ideas. He was arrested during the Stalinist purges, and died in a labor camp in 1944.

Karl Koehler (b. 1913)
Victor Ancona (b. 1912)
joined forces and submitted several entries to the Artists for Victory war poster competition in 1942. The purpose of the competition was to elicit material for propaganda rather than museum-quality art; artists had a choice of eight themes and some twenty slogans. Koehler/Ancona's prizewinning poster, their attempt at portraying the quintessential Nazi, was one version of what proved to be the most popular theme, "This is the Enemy," and one of two-thousand, two-hundred entries to the competition.

Oskar Kokoschka (1886–1980)
whose birthplace was the Austrian village of Pöchlarn on the Danube, spent most of his youth in Vienna and began studies in painting and drawing at the Vienna Kunstgewerbeschule in 1904. He received an invitation to exhibit in the first Vienna Kunstshau, held in 1908. This government-subsidized exhibition was intended to attract tourists and convince the world of Vienna's superiority in the arts. Kokoschka entered posters, drawings, lithographs, sculpture and paintings. The latter entry included work that evoked the fantasy life of dreams, and so shocked and enraged the conservative elements that Kokoschka's stipend at the Kunstgewerbeschule was removed by Alfred Roller, then director of the school. The architect Adolf Loos, a member of the Viennese avant-garde, became Kokoschka's mentor soon after. Under his guidance, Kokoschka began to travel, first to Switzerland and then to Berlin where he gained his second patron and became an illustrator for the journal *Der Sturm*. In 1915–16 Kokoschka fought on the Eastern Front and was severely wounded. After a time of recuperation in Sweden, he taught at the Dresden Academy from 1919 to 1924, but during the succeeding years he traveled extensively, designed stage sets, continued to paint and to write books and plays.

Helmut Kurtz (1903–1959)

Anton Lavinsky (1893–1968)
studied architecture at a technical school in Baku on the Caspian Sea. From 1918 to 1920 he trained at the Petrograd Vkhutemas and transferred to the Saratov branch for the years 1919 and 1920. Working his way toward Moscow, Lavinsky became a professor at the Vkhutemas there in 1920, and was head of the sculpture department for a time. He was also a member of Inkhuk, a group of artists concerned primarily with the theory and definition of Constructivism through research and formal experimentation. Along with the poet and artist Mayakovsky and others, Lavinsky designed ROSTA posters for Moscow buildings. During the 1920s the Soviet government provided financial support for the film industry, as the cinema proved to be an effective educational tool of the Revolution, and Lavinsky designed film posters, among them a promotional piece for Sergei Eisenstein's monumental 1926 film *Battleship Potemkin 1905*.

Bart van der Leck (1876–1958)
was a Dutch painter born in Utrecht. He attended the State School for Decorative Arts in that city and also the Academy in Amsterdam. His posters mirror the development of his painting. His early paintings, like the poster, "Batavier-Lijn," treated their subjects in a very stylized manner. Figures were depicted in flat forms and primary colors, yet maintain a strong representational readability. In 1917 van der Leck joined the De Stijl group and further abstracted his subjects into compositions of lines and geometrical forms. This approach is seen in the "Plantennet Delfia" poster where an image of the salad oil being advertised can be discerned within what at first appears to be a completely abstract work. Although other De Stijl members went on to explore completely nonobjective painting, van der Leck retained his references to figural composition.

El Lissitzky (1890–1941)
was born at Smolensk. He studied architecture in Darmstadt from 1909 to 1914 when he returned to Russia to study in Moscow. In 1915 he began his career practicing architecture, graphic design and painting. In 1919 Lissitzky was appointed Professor of Architecture and Graphic Art at the School of Fine Arts in Vitebsk where he met Malevich, one of the leading figures in Russian modernism. In 1919 he also began a series of constructivist paintings which he called his Proun series. He was also exploring typographical design at this time in his 1920 story "Of 2 Squares." In the same year Lissitzky taught at Vkhutemas in Moscow. In 1922 he went to Berlin where he designed an exhibition that presented modern Russian art to the West for the first time. In Europe, until 1928, Lissitzky was involved in the publication of several modernist periodicals and in contact with leading members of the European avant-garde. Through Moholy-Nagy and Gropius he had an important influence on Bauhaus design. When Lissitzky returned to Russia in 1928 he devoted himself to typography and exhibition design.

Charles Loupot (1892–1962)
studied at the École des Beaux-Arts in Lyons, but worked in lithography and poster design in Switzerland from 1916 until 1923. At that time he moved to Paris and began to design advertisements for such clients as Voisin cars. The establishment of the design studio Alliance Graphique in 1930 brought together the talents of Loupot and Cassandre for a brief time. Commissioned in 1937 to redesign the poster advertising St. Raphael Quinquina, Loupot based his image on an anonymous design depicting two waiters with trays of the aperitif. He produced highly successful variations of a trademark for St. Raphael from 1938 until 1957, first as art director of the firm and later from the Atelier Loupot.

Margaret Macdonald (1865–1933)
Frances Macdonald (1874–1921)
Herbert McNair (1868–1955)
The sisters Margaret and Frances Macdonald met the architect Charles Rennie Mackintosh and his colleague Herbert McNair while studying at the Glasgow School of Art. A similarity of artistic concerns inspired their collaboration. They joined forces in 1893 and became known as "the Four of Glasgow." Their kinship became more than stylistic: McNair wed Frances in 1899 and Margaret and Mackintosh were married the following year. The Four designed posters, book illustrations, metalwork and furniture in a style influenced by Aubrey Beardsley and Jan Toorop. Their own style was more rectilinear and constrained, however. The Macdonald sisters and McNair also introduced symbolist and mystical content into their work as can be seen in the 1895 poster, "The Glasgow Institute of the Fine Arts." A 1900 exhibition in Vienna that included the work of The Four was influential in the evolution of the Secessionist style.

Charles Rennie Mackintosh (1868–1929)
was born in Glasgow, Scotland where he also received his education. As a young man Mackintosh apprenticed to a Glasgow architect and shortly thereafter joined an architectural firm as a draftsman. In the 1890s he worked closely with Margaret and Frances Macdonald and Herbert McNair. The Four together developed the distinctive style of Glasgow Art Nouveau. His graphic design gave greater structure and order to the sinuous lines dominating the Art Nouveau of the Continent. Mackintosh is also important as an early modern architect. His design for the Glasgow School of

Art, completed in 1909, presented fresh architectural values and rejected the eclecticism that dominated the scene. His approach to architectural design included furniture and the overall decoration of the interior. Unappreciated in Glasgow, Mackintosh left in 1914 in the wake of local artistic conservatism and spent his remaining years in England.

Herbert Matter (b. 1901)
studied painting at the École des Beaux-Arts in Geneva from 1925 to 1927 and at the Académie Moderne in Paris, under Léger, in 1928 and 1929. In Paris he worked with A.M. Cassandre on posters, Le Corbusier on architecture and exhibition design and with Deberny and Peignot as a photographer and typographer. He returned to his native Switzerland in 1932 where he designed striking photomontage posters for the Swiss National Tourist Office in Zurich, such as his 1935 "Pontresina Engadin." He reduced complex information to potent, elemental images relying on photography and a minimum of typography. In 1936 Matter settled in New York where he did free-lance photography for *Vogue* and *Harper's Bazaar,* exhibition design for The Museum of Modern Art and advertisements for various agencies. In 1939 he created designs for the New York World's Fair. From 1946 to 1957 he was staff photographer for Condé Nast Publications. He produced the film *Works of Calder* for The Museum of Modern Art in 1949 and was responsible for typography and bookcovers for that institution and for the Guggenheim Museum. In the following decades Matter was a Professor of Photography at Yale University and he has continued to work as a designer.

Vladimir Mayakovsky (1893–1930)
a graduate of the Academy of Fine Arts in Moscow, possessed literary as well as graphic ability. He was a poet and playwright, and together with a circle of artistic and literary friends published a manifesto of Russian Futurism, "A Slap in the Face of Public Taste," late in 1912. His *Mystery-Bouffe,* a play commemorating the first anniversary of the Revolution, was staged in November 1918. Mayakovsky frequently traveled to the West and returned home with samples of art and news of life outside the boundaries of Russia. When he had finished with these materials, such as photographs, magazines and books, he gave them to friends. Rodchenko and Lavinsky were often among the recipients of these links to Paris and other cultural centers of the world. Mayakovsky was one of the creators of the special technique of poster art for ROSTA windows.

Hansjörg Mayer (b. 1943)
studied not only graphic design and composition in his native Stuttgart, but also philosophy with Max Bense at the University of Stuttgart. In 1960 he began producing experimental films and in 1964 started his own publishing company, Edition Hansjörg Mayer. For many years he collaborated with Petersburg Press in London where he now resides. He is an editor, designer and producer of artists' books as well as books on anthropology and ethnology.

C. O. Müller (dates unknown)

Josef Müller-Brockmann (b. 1914)
at Rapperswil, Switzerland, attended the Kunstgewerbeschule in Zurich, opening his studio there in 1936. In 1957 he was named Professor at the Kunstgewerbeschule and in 1959 he founded and became co-editor of *Neue Graphik,* a tri-lingual journal of the Swiss, or International Style. Müller-Brockmann is a leading proponent of this formal style. In 1951 the Tonhalle Gesellschaft, Zurich, commissioned Müller-Brockmann to design its concert posters. The artist has said he intended these designs to be a "symbolic expression of the conformity of music to its inner laws" and that "the proportions of the formal elements and their intermediate spaces are almost always related to certain numerical progressions logically followed out."

Frank Newbould (1887–1951)
received his artistic education at the Bradford College of Art. His pictorialist approach recalls the flat, simple patterning of the Beggarstaffs. Newbould was a favorite designer of the London and North Eastern Railway (L.N.E.R.) in the 1930s, for which he produced many posters. These include several pastel vignettes of the English countryside, often accompanied by fragments of verse, that established a "landscape school" in English poster design of the 30s.

Jayme Odgers (b. 1939)
in Butte, Montana, attended the Art Center School in Los Angeles from 1958 to 1962 on the first full scholarship awarded by that institution. From 1964 to 1966 he had a two-year apprenticeship with Paul Rand. A graphic designer and self-taught photographer, Odgers was one of fifteen artists commissioned by the Olympic Committee to design a poster for the 1984 summer games in Los Angeles.

Josef Maria Olbrich (1867–1908)
studied architecture at the Vienna Academy where he worked under Otto Wagner. He was a co-founder of the Vienna Secession and his building for the Secession, 1897–98, established his architectural reputation. Like Mackintosh, by whom he was influenced, Olbrich gave a firm rectilinear system to the sinuous organic forms that were so prevalent in Art Nouveau design. This style can be seen in Olbrich's 1898 poster illustrating his newly completed exhibition hall for the Secession. The stylized lettering is fanciful but compact and clear. It is included as an element of equal importance to the illustration. The combination of order and ornamentation found in Olbrich's work was attractive to Ernst Ludwig, the Grand Duke of Hesse. In 1899 he called Olbrich to Darmstadt to join the Grand Duke's artists' colony where Olbrich designed several important works including the Wedding Tower, the Studio House and some private houses. His last major building was the Tietz department store in Düsseldorf.

Edward Penfield (1866–1925)
was born in Brooklyn, New York. He attended the Art Students League in New York City, and from 1893 to 1899 Penfield worked exclusively for *Harper's* for which he produced a well-known series of posters. Along with Will Bradley, Penfield is regarded as seminal to the development of the American poster. His style reflects the influence of the French poster designers Toulouse-Lautrec, Steinlen and Bonnard and, like them, Penfield found inspiration in the Japanese print. His designs made use of large, open areas, flat color and unusual viewpoints. They usually depicted only one or two figures that were representative of the gentry. In addition to work for *Harper's, Collier's,* and other clients, Penfield designed posters for forthcoming books.

Nikolai Prusakov (1900–1952)
was a pupil at the Stroganov School in Moscow from 1911 to 1918, in all probability sharing classes with Alexander Rodchenko and the Stenberg brothers, Vladimir and Georgii, at some time during those years. In 1919 and again in 1921 he entered his work in the Obmokhu (Young Constructivist Artists) exhibitions. Prusakov completed studies at Vkhutemas in 1924, and during the mid-20s and early 30s he proved to be a creative and prolific poster designer.

Tom Purvis (1888–1959)
was born in Bristol, England. He studied at Camberwell School of Art and with Degas and Sickert. He worked for an advertising firm for six years before he began his free-lance practice in 1907. His posters were visible in England from 1900 to 1914 but it was not until after World War I that he developed a mature personal style which is exemplified in his posters for the London Underground. Detail was eliminated and a few broad masses of color created images that were the epitome of art deco smartness and sophistication. Purvis also created posters for the L.N.E.R. in which he applied this approach to larger figural compositions. He was a vice president of the Royal Society of Arts and was among the first to receive the R.D.I. (Royal Designer for Industry) established in 1937.

Günter Rambow (b. 1938)
Gerhard Lienemeyer (b. 1936)
Michael van de Sand (b. 1945)
The collaboration between Günter Rambow and Gerhard Lienemeyer began while they were students at the Hochschule für bildende Künste in Kassel. In 1960 they established the Rambow + Lienemeyer Studio. The partners later moved the studio to Stuttgart and then in 1967 they founded a new atelier in Frankfurt. Michael van de Sand became a partner in 1973 and the posters of these three continue to offer surreal images that are arresting visual metaphors. Since 1974 Rambow has been Professor of Graphic Design and Photography at the University of Kassel.

Paul Rand (b. 1914)
is a native of New York City, where he studied at the Pratt Institute, the Art Students League with George Grosz, and at Parsons School of Design. By the time he was thirty-two years old, Rand had published his influential *Thoughts on Design,* a book that continues to edify graphic designers with its approaches to problem solving. Since 1956 he has been a design consultant for such corporations as International Business Machines, Westinghouse and Cummins Engine Co. In 1956 he created an enduring logo for IBM, and later for UPS, Westinghouse and ABC Television. Among his many awards are the gold medal of the American Institute of Graphic Arts, the New York Art Directors Hall of Fame, and an honorary Doctor of Fine Arts from Philadelphia College of Art. Throughout the years Rand has devoted much of his time to design education and has taught at the Cooper Union, Pratt Institute and Yale University.

Man Ray (1890–1977)
was born in Philadelphia, but studied painting in New York City at the Ferrer Center and other schools. During this time he also worked as an advertising artist and later as an engineering draftsman. A friendship with Alfred Stieglitz led to a lifelong interest in photography which began in 1915. He met Marcel Duchamp the same year, and with him and Francis Picabia founded the New York dada movement in 1917. In 1921 he went to Paris where he was a member of Paris dada and, later, the surrealist movement. He is regarded as one of the most important photographers of his time for his explorations into the medium's new possibilities—his "rayograph" technique and the creation of abstract and surreal compositions and effects. His 1932 poster for the London Underground reflects his surrealist experiments in photography. The symbol of the Underground is propelled through space juxtaposed with the planet Saturn, its visual analogue. Man Ray left Paris and returned to America in 1940 to escape Nazi occupation of the French capital. He settled in Hollywood until his return to Paris in 1950.

Paul Renner (1878–1956)
attended art schools in Berlin, Karlsruhe and Munich, and began his career as a painter. His first important job was as a book designer for the Georg Müller publishing company in Munich. From 1926 to 1933 he was Director of the Munich School for Master Book Printers where he appointed Jan Tschichold Lecturer in Typography. Renner was dismissed from his directorship by the National Socialist regime because of his criticism of their policies. Renner is known for his sans-serif Futura typeface, developed in the 1920s. Like other vanguard designs of the 1920s, his 1928 exhibition poster forgoes illustration and makes use of sans-serif letters, a diagonal orientation and abstract geometric forms. Renner is the author of several books and journal articles that address both the practical and aesthetic problems of the printing industry.

Numa Rick (dates unknown)

Alexander Rodchenko (1891–1956)
was born in St. Petersburg where his father was
employed as a stage property craftsman, and
Rodchenko spent the first two decades of his life
in the theatrical world. The family moved to
Kazan not long after his birth, and there he
attended art school. In his early twenties
Rodchenko grew bored with the unprogressive
methods of teaching at the school and left for
Moscow where he took some classes at the
Stroganov School. When World War I erupted
Rodchenko established himself as a free-lance
artist among the avant-garde of Moscow. By
1920 he was an ardent constructivist, and as
head of the metalwork department at
Vkhutemas, he and his students designed such
useful objects as furniture, exhibition stands and
kiosks. From 1922 to 1924 he produced film titles
for Dziga Vertov's documentary newsreels. In
1928 Stalin announced a five-year plan of control
over all activities, including those of the
constructivists, and Rodchenko's work lost much
of the flavor of constructivist principles although
he remained active in typographical design and
photography until his death.

Peter Röhl (b. 1890)
studied in the early part of this century at Berlin's
Royal Museum of Arts and Crafts, and by 1913
was a master student at the Grandducal College
of Fine Arts in Weimar. After serving in World
War I, Röhl returned to Weimar where he met
Walter Gropius and became involved with the
Bauhaus. While Theo van Doesburg was living
in Weimar, Röhl was among those who took a
De Stijl course from him in 1921, and he, along
with several fellow Germans including Max
Burchartz, became an ardent supporter of
De Stijl. Röhl subsequently contributed to the
De Stijl and *Mécano* journals published by van
Doesburg. From 1926 until the late 30s he taught
in Frankfurt, and in 1946 Röhl returned to Kiel,
the city of his birth, to continue painting.

Alfred Roller (1864–1935)
was born in Brno, Czechoslovakia. He studied at
the Academy of Fine Arts in Vienna. He was a
member of the Vienna Secession from its
founding in 1897 until 1905. From 1901 to 1902
he was president of the Union. From 1899 on
Roller taught at the Vienna Kunstgewerbeschule.
Roller was also charged by Gustav Mahler with
the responsibility for the decor of the Vienna
Opera House. His exhibition posters for the
Secession reflect the orderly yet fanciful style of
that school. In the poster for the XVI Exhibition,
Roller allowed the typographic elements to play
the central role. Illustration is absent, the
elongated letters which stand out against an
open background are the decorative focus of the
composition.

Emil Ruder (1914–1970)
was a composer's apprentice in Zurich, the city
of his birth, from 1929 to 1933. He studied under
Walter Käch in 1941–42 at the Zurich
Kunstgewerbeschule and became a typography
instructor himself at the Basel Allgemeine
Gewerbeschule where he taught from 1942 until
1970. Ruder is known for his theory of space as
integral to the message and is the author of
Typography, A Manual of Design, published in
1967. He was co-founder of the International
Center for Typographic Arts (ICTA) in New York.

Yakov Rukhlevsky (1894–1965)
was hired by Goskino (later Sovkino), the film
production and distribution organization for the
Russian Republic in the mid-20s, as an artist-
designer, to head the department responsible
for production of film posters. He organized a
team of young artists (among them were the
Stenbergs and Nikolai Prusakov), and under
Rukhlevsky's supervision the group created
hundreds of dynamic works.

Xanti Schawinsky (1904–1979)
a native of Basel, studied art and architecture in
Zurich, Cologne and Berlin. In 1924 he became
a student at the Bauhaus in Weimar where he
was active in the theater as a designer, writer and
dancer, and acted as assistant to Oskar
Schlemmer. At the Bauhaus in Dessau he taught
stage design and became involved in painting.
He left the Bauhaus in 1929 to direct the graphic
arts studios of the city of Magdeburg. He worked
as a free-lance graphic artist and exhibition
designer in Berlin from 1931 until 1933. In 1933
he left Germany for Italy where he worked as a
designer until 1936 creating photomontage
posters using large images and a minimum of
typography. Schawinsky came to the U.S. in
1936 when Josef Albers invited him to teach at
Black Mountain College in North Carolina. In
1938 he went to New York where he designed
the North Carolina pavilion for the New York
World's Fair.

Fritz Schleifer (dates unknown)
was a German designer and architect. He was a
first generation student at the Bauhaus in
Weimar and designed a poster for the 1923
Bauhaus exhibition that adapts the geometric
profile designed by Oskar Schlemmer as a
symbol of the Bauhaus, to a large-scale, colored
composition.

Oskar Schlemmer (1888–1943)
studied at the Academy of Fine Arts in Stuttgart,
where he was born. He explored dance, relief
sculpture and mural painting during the years
1912 to 1920. In 1920 Gropius appointed
Schlemmer to the staff of the Bauhaus where
he was initially a master of the mural workshop,
and later master of the stone and wood
workshop and the metal workshop. His *Triadic
Ballet* was performed at the Bauhaus exhibition
of 1923 and in the same year he became director
of the Bauhaus stage workshop. When a
typography workshop was established at the
Dessau Bauhaus, Schlemmer was one of those
who carried out work for the department. His
poster for his *Triadic Ballet* illustrates a very
personal approach to design. Schlemmer left the
Bauhaus in 1929 but despite years of harassment
by the Nazis, Schlemmer did not leave Germany.
He struggled on in isolation and poverty in his
remaining years.

Joost Schmidt (1893–1948)
was born in Germany. He studied at the
Academy in Weimar from 1911 to 1914 when he
was called for war service. In 1919 he renewed
his studies at the Weimar Bauhaus,
concentrating on sculpture and typography.
When the Bauhaus moved to Dessau in 1925
Schmidt was appointed head of the sculpture
department and teacher of typography. He later
headed the commercial typography class as
successor to Herbert Bayer. In 1933 Schmidt was
branded a "cultural bolshevik" and lost his
studio, but was again appointed a Professor of
Fine Arts in 1945 in Berlin. Schmidt's poster for
the 1923 Bauhaus exhibition won first prize in a
student competition. Its geometric illustration is
closely integrated with its words. The tense
diagonals and spare colors reflect the influence
of avant-garde Russian design. Schmidt, along
with Bayer and Moholy-Nagy, was responsible
for turning Bauhaus typography away from
Jugendstil and Expressionism toward a
functionalist aesthetic.

Walter Schnackenberg (1880–1961)
was born at Lauterberg, Germany (now
Lauterbourg, France). In 1897 Schnackenberg
went to Munich, the city where he received his
artistic education and which served as home
base throughout much of his career. From 1908
to 1909, however, he worked out of his own
studio in Paris. He established a reputation as a
poster designer before World War I and is also
known for his elegant ballet and theater
costumes. His work was exhibited extensively
beginning in 1905 at the Berlin Secession, and
later at the Munich Secession and in many other
European cities.

Paul Schuitema   (b. 1897)
in Groningen in northern Holland studied at the Academy of Art in Rotterdam from 1916 to 1920. Although his formal training was in painting, he soon concerned himself with graphic design. In the early 1920s he acted as advisor for the Berkel Manufacturing Company for which he designed a trademark, stationery, booklets, showrooms and exhibition stands. Schuitema's essential aesthetic dictated that a design should be "taut and arresting." He relied entirely upon sans-serif type and used only the color red in his black and white designs. Simple abstract elements were sometimes included in his compositions, and in 1926 photography began to play a major role in his work. From 1923 to 1954 he worked in films and taught at the Royal Academy in The Hague from 1930 to 1963.

Schulz-Neudamm   (dates unknown)
was staff designer for motion picture publicity at UFA, Universum-Film Aktiengesellschaft, a major German film studio in operation from 1917 to 1937. His 1926 poster for Fritz Lang's silent film classic, *Metropolis,* illustrates a city of the future in a modernist machine aesthetic. The hand-drawn letters are jagged and sharp, adding a sense of menace to the presence of the robot in the foreground.

Kurt Schwitters   (1887–1948)
studied at the Academy of Dresden, the Berlin Academy and the Technical College in Hanover, the city of his birth, where he was also a student of architecture. He is well-known for his Merz collages, first produced in 1918, creations of paper, glue, paint and found objects that reflect a dadaist outlook. His work was published in Tristan Tzara's dada magazine, *Der Zeltweg,* and Schwitters lectured throughout Europe spreading the dada message. Schwitters maintained a commercial art studio in Hanover where he designed pamphlets, posters and other advertising for a number of clients, including the city of Hanover. In 1929 he worked under Gropius as a typographer for the Dammerstock exhibition in Karlsruhe. His poster for this event demonstrates the sans-serif type and clean composition characteristic of functionalist design of the time. In 1937 Schwitters left Nazi Germany and settled in Oslo, Norway. When Germany invaded Norway in 1940 he escaped to Scotland. He spent his last years in England. Theo van Doesburg (1883–1931) was the founder and chief spokesman for the Dutch-centered De Stijl movement for which he published and edited *De Stijl* magazine, an international journal of art theory and criticism. Van Doesburg was Schwitters's collaborator for the poster "Kleine Dada Soirée."

Mart Stam   (b. 1899)
is a Dutch architect known for playing a key role in the development of functionalism. He worked from 1925 to 1928 with J.A. Brinckmann and L.C. van der Vlucht in Rotterdam, a partnership known primarily for the design of the van Nelle chocolate and tobacco factory. In 1926 Stam was one of fifteen architects invited by Mies van der Rohe to submit designs for the Weissenhof housing estate proposed by the city of Stuttgart. One of the most famous pieces of furniture that Stam created was the tubular steel chair he produced for his three houses on the Weissenhof estate. This enterprise in "modern" living was included as part of the Werkbund exhibition, *die Wohnung,* before the dwellings were released to the city of Stuttgart. In 1930 he emigrated to the Soviet Union, but most of his projects there were unrealized. He later moved between Amsterdam and eastern Europe on several occasions, and eventually became a recluse. Whether he is still living is uncertain, for Stam does not communicate with the outside world.

Vladimir Stenberg   (1899–1982)
Georgii Stenberg   (1900–1933)
were sons of a Swedish father and a Russian mother, who were born in Moscow, but did not become Soviet citizens until 1933. Even at an early age they worked closely together, learning to draw under the tutelage of their father, a painter. Due to illness, Vladimir repeated first grade, and consequently the brothers became classmates who were virtually inseparable. From 1912 to 1917 they attended the Stroganov School in Moscow, and then continued their education at Svomas, the result of combining the Moscow Institute of Painting, Sculpture and Architecture with the Stroganov. From 1922 to 1931 the brothers designed stage sets for the Kamerny Theatre, but finally dissolved the association in order to pursue other artistic activities, particularly the decoration of Red Square which they had begun in 1928. Noteworthy among their stage designs were those for G.B. Shaw's *Saint Joan,* Eugene O'Neill's *The Hairy Ape* and *Desire under the Elms* and Bertolt Brecht's *Beggar's Opera.* In 1925 the Stenbergs received the Gold Medal at the Exposition des Arts Décoratifs in Paris for their accomplishments as theater designers. Together they designed some 300 film posters, and were organizers of the First Film Poster Exhibition at the Kamerny Theatre in 1925. After Georgii's untimely death, Vladimir continued to design posters and array Red Square for special occasions.

Niklaus Stoecklin   (b. 1896)
began his formal training as an artist at the Kunstgewerbeschule in Munich and then in his early 20s returned home to Basel to attend the Allgemeine Gewerbeschule there. The posters he designed soon after his arrival in Basel combined humor and realism and were antecedents of what came to be known as the Basel graphic style. Stoecklin designed advertising posters for such distinguished clients as Burger-Kehl & Co., the Zurich men's clothier, and Valvo lights. He was among the first to win an award for best poster of the year in Switzerland, a competition initiated in 1942 to combat the growing threat to freedom of thought and expression and the resultant decline in the quality of poster design in the early 1940s. Stoecklin received best poster awards for the years 1941, 1942 and 1945. He is also well-known for his ingenious designs for postage stamps commissioned by the Swiss Postal Service.

Ladislav Sutnar   (1897–1976)
was born in Pilsen, Czechoslovakia. After training at Prague's Academy of Applied Arts and Technical University, he established his career in that city where he was an advocate of functional design and the Bauhaus ideal. He was Professor of Design and Director of the State School for Graphic Arts in Prague from the mid-1920s until 1939 when he came to the United States as Exhibition Director for the Czech Pavilion of the 1939 New York World's Fair. Sutnar remained in New York and in 1941 became Art Director of Sweet's Catalog Service. In 1951 he headed his own design firm and was Art Director of *Theatre Arts* magazine.

Horace Taylor   (1881–1934)
was a painter, poster artist and stage designer who worked primarily in his native London. In 1898 he studied at Camden School of Art, then took classes at the Royal Academy Schools in 1902. He attended the Munich Royal Academy in 1905. Taylor worked as a cartoonist for the *Manchester Guardian* and after 1922 he concentrated his efforts in the field of commercial art.

Karel Teige (1900–1950)
studied philosophy and art history at Charles University in his native Prague. His interest in the arts later manifested itself in the many typographical poster designs that he produced during the late 1920s, and through the journal *Stavba,* for which he was editor from 1923 until 1931. Teige was an influential spokesman for functionalism. In 1930 he lectured at the Dessau Bauhaus on sociology and architecture.

Georg Trump (b. 1896)
in the city of Brettheim, Germany, was enrolled in the Stuttgart State Academy of Arts and Crafts when World War I brought his education to a temporary halt. Trump resumed his studies after the war, graduated in 1923 and spent three years in Italy as a painter and ceramist. In 1926 he joined the staff of the Kunstgewerbeschule in Bielefeld, and Trump designed a poster for a 1927 exhibition at the school. He continued his teaching as a typography instructor in Munich from 1929 to 1931. He spent the next three years at the East Berlin College of Arts and Crafts, and eventually settled in Munich where, from 1934 to 1953, he was head of the School for Master Book Printers, succeeding Paul Renner. In 1953 he established a free-lance design practice and from then on worked primarily on the creation of new typefaces.

Jan Tschichold (1902–1974)
inherited an interest in lettering from his father who was a type designer. He studied calligraphy at the Academy of Book Design in Leipzig, where he was born. In 1923 he visited the Bauhaus exhibition in Weimar and was profoundly impressed. In 1925 Tschichold began his influential writings on typography. Through numerous articles and several books he introduced the principles of "the new typography" to a wide audience that included practical printers as well as avant-garde artists. He advocated a functionalist aesthetic; economy of expression, sans-serif type and asymmetrical composition. He was also early to recognize the importance of photography as a design tool in advertising. All these elements can be seen in a series of Phoebus-Palast cinema posters where photography was used in film promotion. In 1926 Paul Renner appointed Tschichold to the faculty of the Munich School for Master Book Printers where he taught typography and lettering until 1933, when he emigrated to Switzerland to escape Nazi oppression. Shortly thereafter, he began to see parallels between "the new typography" and National Socialism: both were uncompromising in their discipline

and restrictiveness. By 1935 Tschichold had returned to a more traditional typographic style and saw "the new typography" as an alternative, not an absolute. In 1947 Tschichold was invited to England to revise the typographical design of Penguin Books.

Tristan Tzara (1896–1963)
was Rumanian by birth. He studied at the University in Zurich where he played a central role in the birth of dada at the Cabaret Voltaire. He was primarily a poet and explored sound poetry, nonsense poetry and the poetry of chance with Hugo Ball, Richard Huelsenbeck and Jean Arp in dada performances and publications. In 1917 he began to edit the periodical *DADA.* His theories are expressed in his "Seven Manifestos of Dada," written in 1924. Tzara moved to Paris in 1921 to participate in the dada movement there. He soon became a leader of a divisive faction opposed to those led by André Breton and Francis Picabia. Tzara's 1921 poster for the "Salon Dada," an exhibition that closed the "Saison Dada 1921," applies dada's rebellion against convention to typographical design. His words are created from both upper and lowercase letters of different typefaces and the individual letters are placed freely in the composition, giving the work a feeling of spontaneity and vitality which is characteristic of dada design.

Ben Vautier (b. 1935)
lives in Nice, France, and has been a participant in the major movements coming out of dada, among them Fluxus. In 1962 he met George Maciunus, one of the Fluxus organizers, while Maciunus was traveling in Europe. They organized the Festival Mondial Fluxus et Art Total in Nice in 1963. The following year Vautier performed Fluxus street theater in New York. In one such "performance" on Canal Street, Vautier, seated and wrapped in string, played the violin with a stethoscope. Vautier is also a painter, writer and publisher.

Henry van de Velde (1863–1957)
was born in Antwerp, Belgium and trained there as a painter. Through contact with the work of Jules Chéret and the English Arts and Crafts movement, van de Velde began to work in graphic design in 1892. He sought a style free from the past and found it in the flat patterns and resilient curves of the Art Nouveau. Van de Velde's poster for Tropon, a food processing company, is one of a number of designs done for the firm which included trademarks and packaging as well as posters. Tropon's hiring of an artist to supervise its design was precedent setting in the establishment of the modern design professions. Van de Velde was also

known for his furniture and interior design and in 1901 he was called to Weimar where he became head of the Kunstgewerbeschule. There, moving away from Art Nouveau, he was influential in promoting the elimination of ornament, the relevance of the nature of materials, the potential of machine production and a creative and experimental approach to architecture and design. In 1911 when van de Velde resigned, he recommended Walter Gropius as his successor, thus playing a crucial role in the formation of the Bauhaus which was born when the Kunstgewerbeschule reorganized after World War I.

Massimo Vignelli (b. 1931)
studied architecture in Milan and Venice, and then began working with his wife, Lella, an architect. Although the Vignellis moved their firm from Milan to New York in 1965, they continue to work for major European companies and institutions. They have provided corporate identities for such clients as American Airlines and Bloomingdale's; for Knoll International they designed a corporate graphic program. Other projects have included sign systems for the Washington Metro and the New York Subways. Among their many awards is the 1983 Gold Medal of the American Institute of Graphic Arts. Mr. Vignelli has taught and lectured on design in major universities in the U.S. and abroad.

M. Wechsler (dates unknown)

Wolfgang Weingart (b. 1941)
learned the craft of hot-metal typesetting as an apprentice and is a self-taught designer. Since 1968 he has been an instructor of typography at the Basel Allegemeine Gewerbeschule. He also teaches a typography course annually for the Yale Summer Program in Graphic Design, Brissago, Switzerland. *Projects*, a study of the work of two of his students, was published in 1980. He continues to lecture in Europe and the U.S., and to create typography in his uniquely iconoclastic style.

Hendrikus Wijdeveld (b. 1885)
in The Hague, began working in architectural offices in Amsterdam at the age of twelve. In 1905 Wijdeveld went to England to study the works of Morris and Ruskin. While there he worked in the offices of a London architectural firm and attended evening classes at the Lambeth School of Art. In 1911 he went to France where he worked until 1913 in Lille and Paris for the architect Cordonnier. In 1914 he returned to Holland where he started his own practice, receiving commissions for country houses, theaters, shops, interiors and working class apartments. In 1918 he founded the magazine *Wendingen,* published until 1931. This was the vehicle through which Wijdeveld established his reputation as advocate of the Amsterdam School, an expressionist movement in architecture that was opposed to the De Stijl group. Wijdeveld was responsible for the content and design of *Wendingen.* His "Wijdeveld typeface," large, ornamental letters and decorative borders became known as "the Wendingen style" which was influential in Holland for a number of years. Wijdeveld's posters illustrate these characteristics as well as his frequent use of rectangular blocks of text that alternate with blank blocks. His 1931 Frank Lloyd Wright exhibition poster also underscores the influence Wijdeveld had in bringing the work of that American architect to the attention of the European public through exposure in *Wendingen.*

Robert J. Wildhack (b. 1881)
was an American designer, illustrator and painter. He was born in Illinois and studied with Robert Henri in New York. His shorthand style of illustration, seen in his 1907 poster for *Scribner's,* is similar to the approach being explored by Germany's Ludwig Hohlwein at about the same time. Wildhack said that "a poster can give no more than the spirit or atmosphere of the subject."

Tadanori Yokoo (b. 1936)
received the Japanese Advertising Artists Club Prize when he was in his early twenties, and from 1961 to 1975 was the recipient of numerous awards from the Tokyo Art Directors' Club. In 1960 he joined the Nippon Design Center and was responsible for the advertising commissioned by such clients as Asahi Breweries, Ltd. At Nippon, Yokoo became acquainted with the poet Takahashi, employed there as a copywriter, and Takahashi introduced Yokoo to the seamy side of Tokyo life that had a direct influence on the development of Yokoo's style. Yokoo left Nippon in 1964 to work as a free-lance artist and poster designer, and he began to incorporate "pop" images into his art. In late 1965 he was one of sixteen designers who participated in an exhibition of a personal nature: the artists themselves were the main theme of the works, and for this exhibition Yokoo produced a poster reflecting, perhaps, his stylistic death and rebirth.

Ilia Zdanevitch (1894–1975)
son of a French father and a Russian mother, was born in Tiflis, now the capital of the Georgian Soviet Socialist Republic. In 1911 Zdanevitch learned of Marinetti's "Manifesto of Futurism" through a friend of the family, the painter Boris Lopatinski. Later that year Zdanevitch enrolled in St. Petersburg University to study law and began to establish himself in avant-garde circles. His futurist manifesto was delivered in 1912 opposing official art and Zdanevitch became renowned as a Russian futurist. At the age of nineteen under the name Eli Eganbyuri he published a book on the rayonist painters Natalya Goncharova and Mikhail Larionov, still considered the best study of their early work. Zdanevitch apprenticed as a typographer from 1918–19 and in 1920 received a scholarship to study in France. After arriving in Paris he quickly made friends with the dadaists and later earned a living by painting scarves with Sonia and Robert Delaunay. During the late 20s and early 30s he worked for Coco Chanel directing fabric production for her firm, and by 1938 he had formed a friendship with Picasso. Two years later he published a book containing six Picasso etchings, and from 1939 to 1974 Zdanevitch produced twenty illustrated works, most of which contained his poetic texts.

Piet Zwart (1885–1977)
was born in Zaandijk, Holland. From 1902 to 1907 he studied at the Amsterdam School of Arts and Crafts where he began the study of architecture. In 1911 he received his first commissions for interior and furniture design. In 1913 he entered the Delft Technical College but his studies were ended in 1914 with the onset of World War I. Zwart made contact with members of De Stijl in 1919 and was influenced by them without wholeheartedly joining them. In 1919 he worked as an assistant to Jan Wils, a De Stijl architect, and in 1921 he became assistant to H.P. Berlage. Through a chance introduction by Berlage, Zwart received a commission to design brochures. Thus it was not until he was thirty-six that he entered the field of typography. He independently developed a style that corresponds almost exactly to that of El Lissitzky, whom he met in 1923. This style can be seen in the purely typographical poster of 1923 in which Zwart abandoned symmetry and introduced lines that lead the eye through the text and large letters and heavy type that arrest the eye. In 1926 Zwart began to use the camera, and soon photographs and photomontage became an integral part of his conception of typography, as can be seen in his 1928 film festival poster.

Bibliography

Books

Abdy, Jane. *The French Poster: Chéret to Cappiello.* New York: Clarkson N. Potter, Inc., 1969.

Allner, W.H. *Posters.* New York: Reinhold Publishing Corporation, 1952.

Barnicoat, John. *A Concise History of the Poster.* London: Thames and Hudson, 1972.

Bojko, Szymon. *New Graphic Design in Revolutionary Russia.* London: Lund Humphries, 1972.

Brattinga, Pieter and Dooijes, Dick. *A History of the Dutch Poster 1890–1960.* Amsterdam: Scheltema & Holkema, 1968.

Fern, Alan and Constantine, Mildred. *Word and Image.* New York: Museum of Modern Art, 1968.

Gerstner, Karl and Kutter, Markus. *The New Graphic Art.* Teufen: Arthur Niggli Ltd., 1959.

Hillier, Bevis. *Posters.* New York: Stein and Day, 1969.

Hillman, Hans and Rambow, Günter. *Ein Plakat ist eine Fläche die ins Auge Springt: Plakate der Kasseler Schule.* Frankfurt: Zweitausendeins, 1979.

Hollmann, Helga, Malhotra, Ruth, Pilipczuk, Alexander, Prignitz, Helga and Thon, Christina. *Das frühe Plakat in Europa und den USA* Band 3. Deutschland. Berlin: Gebr. Mann Verlag, 1980.

Kauffer, E. McKnight. *The Art of the Poster.* London: Cecil Palmer, 1924.

Kepes, Gyorgy. *Language of Vision.* Chicago: Paul Theobald and Co., 1944.

Kossatz, Horst-Herbert. *Ornamental Posters of the Vienna Secession.* London: Academy Editions, 1974.

Kowalski, Tadeusz. *The Polish Film Poster.* Warsaw: Filmowa Agencja Wydawnicza, 1957.

Lyakhov, V. *Soviet Advertising Poster 1917–1932.* Moscow: Soviet Khudozhnik, 1972.

——————. *Soviet Advertisement Poster and Advertisement Graphic 1933–1973.* Moscow: Soviet Khudozhnik, 1977.

Maindron, Ernest. *Les Affiches Illustrées.* Paris: H. Launette and Cie., 1886.

——————. *Les Affiches Illustrées 1886–1895.* Paris: G. Boudet, 1896.

Malhotra, Ruth and Thon, Christina. *Das frühe Plakat in Europa und den USA* Band 1. Grossbritannien Vereinigte Staaten von Nordamerika. Berlin: Gerb. Mann Verlag, 1973.

Malhotra, Ruth, Rinkleff, Marjan and Schälicke, Bernd. *Das frühe Plakat in Europa und den USA* Band 2. Frankreich und Belgien. Berlin: Gebr. Mann Verlag, 1977.

Mascha, Dr. Ottokar. *Österreichische Plakatkunst.* Vienna: Kunstverlag J. Löwy, c. 1910.

Mellinghoff, Frieder. *Kunst-Ereignisse: Plakat zu Kunst.* Ausstellungen. Dortmund: Harenberg Kommunikation, 1978.

Menegazzi, Luigi. *Il Manifesto Italiano 1882–1925.* Milan: Electa Editrice, n.d.

Müller-Brockmann, Josef and Shizuko. *History of the Poster.* Zurich: ABC Verlag, 1971.

Neumann, Eckhard. *Functional Graphic Design in the 20's.* New York, Amsterdam, London: Reinhold Publishing Company, 1967.

Oostens-Wittamer, Yolande. *La Belle Epoque: The Art of the Poster.* n.p.: Grossman Publishers, Inc., 1970.

Poupard-Lieussou, Y. and Sanouillet, M. *Documents Dada.* Geneva: Librairie Weber, 1974.

Price, Charles Matlack. *Poster Design.* New York: George W. Bricka, 1913 (new and enlarged edition 1922).

Rademacher, Hellmut. *Das deutsche Plakat: Von den Anfängen bis zur Gegenwart.* Dresden: VEB Verlag der Kunst, 1965.

——————. *Masters of German Poster Art.* Leipzig: Edition Leipzig, 1966.

Raffe, W.G. *Poster Design.* Pelham: Bridgman Publishers, 1929.

Ruben, Paul. *Die Reklame: ihre Kunst und Wissenschaft.* Volume I. Berlin: Verlag Für Sozialpolitik, 1913.

——————. *Die Reklame: ihre Kunst und Wissenschaft.* Volume II. Berlin: Hermann Paetel Verlag, 1914.

Ruder, Emil. *Typography: A Manual of Design.* Teufen: Verlag Arthur Niggli, 1967.

Schindler, Herbert. *Monografie des Plakate.* München: Süddeutscher Verlag, 1972.

Schmutzler, Robert. *Art Nouveau.* New York: Harry N. Abrams, Inc., 1978.

Schubert, Dr. Walter F. *Die Deutsche Werbe Graphik.* Berlin: Verlag Francken & Lang, 1927.

Seht her, Genossen! Plakate aus der Sowjetunion. Dortmund: Harenberg Kommunikation, 1982.

Sparrow, Walter Shaw. *Advertising and British Art.* London: John Lane and the Bodley Head Limited, 1924.

Spencer, Herbert. *Pioneers of Modern Typography.* London: Lund Humphries Publishers Limited, 1969.

Sponsel, Jean Louis. *Das moderne Plakat.* Dresden: Gerhard Kühtmann, 1897.

Wember, Paul. *die Jugend der Plakate 1887–1917.* Krefeld: Scherpe Verlag, 1961.

Monographs

Herbert Bayer. Das Künstlerische Werk 1918–1938. Berlin: Bauhaus-Archiv, 1982.

Bayer, Herbert (preface). *Yusaku Kamekura: His Works.* n.p.: Bijutsu Shuppan-sha, 1971.

Peter Behrens. *Monographien Deutscher Reklame-Künstler* Band 5. Dortmund: Druck und Verlag von Fr. Wilh. Ruhfus, 1913.

Lucian Bernhard. Monographien Deutscher Reklame-Künstler Band 4. Dortmund: Gedruckt und verlegt bei Fr. Wilh. Ruhfus, 1913.

Bie, Oskar. *Schnackenberg: Kostume/Plakate und Dekorationen.* München: Musarion Verlag, 1922.

Lo Studio Boggeri 1933–1981. Milan: Gruppo Editoriale Electa, 1981.

Broido, Lucy. *The Posters of Jules Chéret.* New York: Dover Publications, Inc., 1980.

Brown, Robert K. and Reinhold, Susan. *The Poster Art of A.M. Cassandre.* New York: E.P. Dutton, 1979.

Celant, Germano. *Marcello Nizzoli.* Milan: Edizioni di Comunità, 1968.

Curci, Roberto. *Marcello Dudovich.* Trieste: Edizioni Lint, 1976.

(Deffke, Wilhelm). Hinkefuss, Carl Ernst. *10 Jahre Deutsch Werbegraphik.* Charlottenburg: Verlag der Internatio, 1923.

F.H. Ehmcke and Clare Ehmcke. Herausgegeben von Deutschen Museum für Kunst in Handelund Gewerbe, Band 1 and Band 2. Dortmund: Verlag Fr. Wilh. Ruhfus, 1911.

Elliott, David (ed.). *Rodchenko and the Arts of Revolutionary Russia.* New York: Pantheon Books, 1979.

Frenzel, Professor H.K. *Ludwig Hohlwein.* Berlin: Phönix Illustrationsdruck und Verlag, 1926.

Fukuda, Shigeo. *Posters of Shigeo Fukuda.* Tokyo: Mitumura Tosho Shuppers Co., Ltd., 1982.

Haworth-Booth, Mark. *E. McKnight Kauffer: A Designer and His Public.* London: Gordon Fraser, 1974.

Herzfelde, Wieland. *John Heartfield Leben und Werk.* Dresden: VEB Verlag der Kunst, 1962.

Max Huber Progetti Grafici 1936–1981. Milan: Gruppo Editoriale Electa, 1982.

Kamekura, Yusaku (ed.). *Paul Rand: His Work from 1946–1958.* Tokyo: Zokeisha Publications Ltd., 1959.

Neuburg, Hans. *Hans Neuburg 50 Anni di Grafica Costruttiva.* Milano: Gruppo Editoriale Electa, 1982.

Sutnar, Ladislav. *Visual Design in Action: Principles, Purposes.* New York: Hastings House, 1961.

Tschichold, Jan. *Leben und Werk des Typographen.* Dresden: VEB Verlag der Kunst, 1977.

Exhibition Catalogues

L'Affiche Anglaise: Les Années 90. Paris: Musée des Arts Décoratifs, 1972.

Jean Carlu. Paris: Musée de l'Affiche, 1980.

Depero: Arte Pubblicitaria. Museo Depero. Folgaria: Edizioni Magnifica Communistà di Folgaria, 1979.

Images of an Era: The American Poster 1945–1975. Washington, D. C.: National Collection of Fine Arts, 1975.

Japanische Plakate Heute. Zurich: Kunstgewerbemuseum, 1979.

Ernst Keller Graphiker 1891–1968 Gesamtwerk. Zurich: Kunstgewerbemuseum, 1976.

Kulturelle Plakate der Schweiz. Zurich: Kunstgewerbemuseum, 1974.

Charles Loupot. Paris: Musée de l'Affiche, n.d.

Majakovskij-Mejerchol'd Stanislavskiji. Venezia: Electa Editrice, 1975.

Mavignier Plakat. Hamburg: Museum für Kunst und Gewerbe, 1981.

Mucha 1860–1939. Grand Palais. Paris: Editions de la Réunion de musée nationaux, 1980.

Plakat Rewolucyjny 1917–1967. Warsaw: Lenin Museum, n.d.

Hernandez, Antonio. *Emil Ruder: Lehrer und Typograph.* Basel: Schriften des Gewerbemuseums, Nr. 10, 1971.

Albe Steiner: Communicazione Visiva. Firenze: Fratelli Alinari SpA Istituto di Edizioni Artistiche, 1977.

Hernandez, A. and His, H.P. *Niklaus Stöcklin.* Basel: Schriften des Gewerbemuseums, Nr. 2, 1966.

Tendenzen der Zwanziger Jahre. Berlin: Neuen Nationalgalerie, der Akademie der Künste und der Grossen Orangerie der Schlosses Charlottenburg zu Berlin, 1977.

Werbestil 1930–1940. Die alltägliche Bildersprache eines Jahrzehnts. Zurich: Kunstgewerbemuseum, 1981.

Piet Zwart. Den Haag: Haags Gemeentemuseum, n.d.

Periodicals

Art and Industry. London, New York: October 1922–December 1958; October 1922–December 1931 as *Commercial Art and Industry;* July 1936–December 1958, *Art and Industry.*

Art et Métiers Graphiques. Paris: Art et Métiers Graphiques. 1927–1939.

Gebrausgraphik-International Advertising Art. Berlin: Phönix Illustrationsdruck und Verlag. 1925–current.

International Poster Biennale. Warsaw: Ministry of Culture and Art and the Polish Artists and Designers Association, nos. 1–8. 1966–1980.

Lahti Poster Biennale. Lahti: Lahti Art Museum, nos. 1–5. 1975–current.

Das Plakat. (Sachs, Hans, ed.) Berlin: Vereins der Plakatfreunde. 1909–1921. (From 1909–1912 known as *Vereins der Plakatfreunde.*)

Poster and Art Collector. London: Vols. 1–6, June 1898–May 1901. From (1898–1900 known as *Poster; an illustrated Monthly Chronicle.*)

Die Reklame. Berlin: Verband deutscher reklamefachleute. Vol. 1–25, no. 16. 1907–1932.

Typographica. (Spencer, Herbert, ed.) London: Lund Humphries. Published irregularly, no. 1–16, 1958–1959; new series no. 1–16, June 1960–December 1967.

Lenders to the Exhibition

Merrill C. Berman
Chermayeff & Geismar Associates, New York, New York
Seymour Chwast/Pushpin Lubalin Peckolick, Inc.,
New York, New York
Arthur A. Cohen
Elaine Lustig Cohen
Inge Druckrey
Ex Libris, New York, New York
Fischer Fine Art, Ltd., London, England
Barry Friedman, Ltd., New York, New York
Daniel Friedman
April Greiman
Robert Jensen
Kunstgewerbemuseum der Stadt Zürich,
Museum für Gestaltung, Zurich, Switzerland
Musei Civici di Rovereto, Galleria Museo Depero,
Rovereto, Italy
Museum of Art, The Pennsylvania State University,
University Park, Pennsylvania
The Museum of Modern Art, New York, New York
Susan J. Pack
Günter Rambow, Gerhard Lienemeyer, Michael van de Sand
Paul Rand
Reinhold-Brown Gallery, New York, New York
W. Michael Sheehe
Thomas Strong
Victoria and Albert Museum, London, England
Walker Art Center
Wolfgang Weingart

Acknowledgments

The 20th-century poster, widely seen but little understood, has generally not received the serious attention it deserves from scholars or collectors. This form's proliferation in the early part of the century and its overt role in commerce has led to the popular view that posters are simply sales tools with little or no value beyond that. (This attitude has also led to the recent development of a kind of non-poster—the so-called "art poster"—a form that falls somewhere between the traditional poster and the contemporary print, but it is neither one nor the other.) Our concern here is exclusively with the poster that communicates a message, a message that may be cultural, political or commercial, in graphic works that are designed to persuade, to sell an idea or a product. Whether pictorial or symbolic, these images reflect an awareness of and on occasion influences from other art forms. These are inventive images—the forms of the avant-garde.

The exhibition would not have been organized without our introduction, three years ago, to Merrill Berman, whose posters constitute the majority of works in it. Mr. Berman's enthusiasm for and knowledge of the 20th-century poster have made his a remarkable, unique collection. Arthur and Elaine Lustig Cohen, who initially put us on the trail of the avant-garde poster, have also made generous loans to the exhibition. Susan Reinhold and Robert Brown, of the Reinhold-Brown Gallery, have contributed vast amounts of time, energy and knowledge to this endeavor. In addition to Robert Brown's essay on the turn of the century poster, he and Susan Reinhold provided the bibliography for this volume, and a number of very critical loans to the exhibition.

Our thanks are extended to all of the other lenders, each of whom has agreed to do without for a rather long period of time so that a wide audience may see and understand this graphic form. Particular gratitude is due the print staff of the Victoria and Albert Museum, especially Margaret Timmers, who gave a good deal of time to me in that extraordinary collection. Stewart Johnson and Robert Coates of The Museum of Modern Art Design Department spent a number of days searching out loan requests and acquainting me with that museum's great poster collection.

The authors of the essays included here have devoted enormous effort and time to their texts. I am especially grateful to Alma Law who not only provided an excellent piece on the Russian film poster but also spent a number of days in interviews with Merrill Berman and in translating the Russian poster texts for this book. Dawn Ades has written an extensive essay on the posters that make up the largest segment of this exhibition: those of the first three decades of the century. In it she has investigated a number of little known areas significant in this as yet incomplete history, and she has developed a number of theses about the evolution of the 20th-century poster that are certain to stimulate controversy and further investigation. Armin Hofmann has contributed the designer's view from the standpoint of one who has produced some of the most compelling recent images in this medium.

Each of the non-English texts has been translated for inclusion in this book, because in the interpretation of posters, the verbal and visual messages are of equal importance. In addition to the Russian translations by Mrs. Law, the German and Dutch posters were translated by Russell Christensen, the French by William Horrigan, the Czech by Sasha Cervenka. The biographies were researched and written by Deborah Leuchovius and Linda Krenzin who, with a few exceptions, were able to unearth material on even the most obscure designers.

Wolfgang Weingart, in addition to lending one of his most recent posters, designed the poster for this exhibition. Our thanks also to George Roos who photographed the majority of the works for this book, and to Mark Magowan and Dana Cole of Abbeville Press for their assistance in its publication.

Art Center graphic designers Robert Jensen and Donald Bergh provided the design for this book and many valuable insights about the works that are included in it. The assistance of other staff members is gratefully acknowledged; their specific roles are listed opposite.

On behalf of the Art Center Board of Directors and staff I want to thank David Brown of Champion International for his enthusiastic support of the exhibition and for that company's financial assistance toward its realization. Support was also provided by a grant from the National Endowment for the Arts Design Arts Program.

Mildred Friedman
Design Curator

Index

Reproduction Credits

Courtesy Albright-Knox Art Gallery: p. 68 (bottom)
Courtesy Seymour Chwast/Pushpin Lubalin Peckolick, Inc.: p. 187 (right)
Courtesy Courtauld Institute of Art, University of London: p. 25
Courtesy Fischer Fine Art, Ltd.: p. 107 (right)
Courtesy Barry Friedman, Ltd.: p. 18
Courtesy Solomon R. Guggenheim Museum: p. 53 (top)
Courtesy Mark Haworth-Booth: p. 68 (top)
Courtesy Kunstgewerbemuseum der Stadt Zürich, Museum für Gestaltung: pp. 134, 146
Courtesy Musei Civici di Rovereto, Galleria Museo Depero: p. 144 (right)

Courtesy Museum of Art, The Pennsylvania State University: p. 107 (left)
Courtesy The Museum of Modern Art, New York: pp. 20, 52 (right), 90, 115 (right), 120 (left), 129, 144 (left), 147 (right), 157 (right), 166 (left), 171 (right), 172, 174, 177 (right), 180, 184
Courtesy Rambow, Lienemeyer, van de Sand: pp. 188, 189
George Roos, courtesy Arthur A. and Elaine Lustig Cohen: pp. 37, 74, 119, 120 (right), 125 (left), 145 (left)
George Roos, courtesy Ex Libris: p. 38
George Roos, courtesy Susan J. Pack: pp. 156, 158, 159 (left), 162 (left), 170
George Roos, courtesy Reinhold-Brown Gallery: pp. 26, 92, 114, 115 (left), 151 (left), 171 (left), 178, 179, 182, back cover
George Roos, courtesy W. Michael Sheehe: p. 173 (left)
Courtesy J. P. Smid, Kunsthandel Monet: p. 42 (top)
Courtesy Stedelijk Van Abbemuseum, Eindhoven, The Netherlands: p. 11
Courtesy Victoria and Albert Museum, Crown Copyright: pp. 110, 112, 117, 149, 168 (right), 169
Walker Art Center: p. 185
Walker Art Center, courtesy Ivan Chermayeff: p. 187 (left)
Walker Art Center, courtesy Inge Druckrey: p. 193
Walker Art Center, courtesy Daniel Friedman: p. 190
Walker Art Center, courtesy April Greiman: p. 191
Walker Art Center, courtesy Mobil Oil Corporation: p. 186
Walker Art Center, courtesy Paul Rand: p. 183
Walker Art Center, courtesy Thomas Strong: p. 181
Courtesy Wolfgang Weingart: pp. 12, 192

Travel Schedule

Walker Art Center
Minneapolis, Minnesota
12 May–12 August 1984

Everson Museum of Art of Syracuse and Onondaga County
Syracuse, New York
8 September–20 October 1984

The Saint Louis Art Museum
St. Louis, Missouri
24 November 1984–5 January 1985

Dayton Art Institute
Dayton, Ohio
6 April–18 May 1985

Neuberger Museum
State University of New York at Purchase
23 June–25 August 1985

The Montreal Museum of Fine Arts
Montreal, Quebec, Canada
26 September–10 November 1985